FURNITURE BY WENDELL CASTLE

FURNITURE BY WENDELL CASTLE

Davira S. Taragin
Edward S. Cooke, Jr.
Joseph Giovannini

Hudson Hills Press, New York
In Association with the Founders Society Detroit Institute of Arts

EXHIBITION ITINERARY

Detroit Institute of Arts
Detroit, Michigan
December 5, 1989–February 4, 1990

Delaware Art Museum
Wilmington, Delaware
March 9–May 13, 1990

Virginia Museum of Fine Arts
Richmond, Virginia
June 19– August 19, 1990

**Memorial Art Gallery
University of Rochester**
Rochester, New York
November 17, 1990–January 20, 1991

American Craft Museum
New York
February 14–April 30, 1991

The exhibition was made possible with the assistance of an anonymous donor and David Schwarz. Additional support was provided by the state of Michigan, the city of Detroit, and the Founders Society.

First Edition

© 1989 by the Founders Society Detroit Institute of Arts.
All rights reserved under International and Pan-American Copyright Conventions.
Published in the United States by Hudson Hills Press, Inc., Suite 1308, 230 Fifth Avenue, New York, NY 10001-7704.

Distributed in the United States, its territories and possessions, Canada, Mexico, and Central and South America by Rizzoli International Publications, Inc.
Distributed in the United Kingdom, Eire, Europe, Israel, and the Middle East by Phaidon Press Limited.
Distributed in Japan by Yohan (Western Publications Distribution Agency).

FOR THE FOUNDERS SOCIETY DETROIT INSTITUTE OF ARTS
Director of Publications: Julia Henshaw
Editor: Cynthia Newman Helms

FOR HUDSON HILLS PRESS
Editor and Publisher: Paul Anbinder
Senior Editor: Virginia Wageman
Indexer: Gisela S. Knight
Designer: Abby Goldstein
Composition: Trufont Typographers
Manufactured in Japan by Toppan Printing Company

Library of Congress Cataloguing-in-Publication Data
  Giovannini, Joseph.
    Furniture by Wendell Castle / Joseph Giovannini, Davira S. Taragin, Edward S. Cooke, Jr.—1st ed.
      p. cm.
    Essays to accompany the first retrospective exhibition of Wendell Castle's work, to be held at the Detroit Institute of Arts, Dec. 6, 1989–Feb. 4, 1990, and 4 other museums, Mar. 2, 1990–Apr. 28, 1991.
    Bibliography: p.
    Includes index.
    1. Castle, Wendell, 1932– —Exhibitions. 2. Furniture—United States—History—20th century—Exhibitions. I. Castle, Wendell, 1932– . II. Taragin, Davira Spiro. III. Cooke, Edward S.
IV. Detroit Institute of Arts. V. Title.
NK2439.C3A4   1989
749.213—dc20   LC 89-83703
                                                              CIP

ISBN: 1-55595-032-9 (alk. paper)

Frontispiece
Wendell Castle standing under *Full Moon*, 1988.

CONTENTS

COLORPLATES

It can be argued that the decorative arts exercise a more profound influence over every aspect of our lives than those arts once designated as "fine." Since the late nineteenth century, Michigan has been an important center for design, noted especially for educational institutions such as the Cranbrook Academy of Art, the contributions of the Pewabic Pottery in Detroit, furniture manufacturing in Grand Rapids in the western part of the state, and the wide-ranging influence of the automobile industry. The Detroit Institute of Arts has presented a number of significant exhibitions on both industrial design and the crafts, among them "An Exhibition for Modern Living" in 1949, "Arts and Crafts in Detroit 1906–1976: The Movement, The Society, The School" in 1976, "Design in America: The Cranbrook Vision" in 1983, and "The Automobile and Culture—Detroit Style" in 1985.

Michigan is proud of its large community of nationally recognized craftspeople working in clay, glass, metal, fiber, and wood; the interest here among artists and collectors in the Studio Craft movement is also high. It is, therefore, most appropriate that the Detroit Institute of Arts organize this exhibition of the work of the important contemporary craftsman Wendell Castle. Castle is one of the pivotal figures in the Studio Craft movement, and it is to be hoped that this exhibition and catalogue will allow his work to be widely seen across America and understood in the context of a movement that cannot be ignored in any comprehensive understanding of the diversity of American art in the late twentieth century. The museum's strong commitment to the acquisition and display of contemporary studio crafts began in 1981 when a significant group of blown glass forms by Dale Chihuly was acquired. In 1988 a major step in this commitment was made with the awarding of a commission for seating in the museum's modern art galleries to Wendell Castle, an effort funded by the Art of Poland Associates, an auxiliary of the Founders Society of the Detroit Institute of Arts.

Castle's work spans the areas of industrial design, craft, and sculpture and thus accurately reflects the diversity of approach that is increasingly characteristic of the successful twentieth-century artist. His sense of humor, his respect for both historical and recent styles, and his immaculate craftsmanship add to the ways his pieces may be enjoyed.

Many individuals are involved in the creation of an exhibition. I would like to take this opportunity to mention specifically some of those who gave generously of their time and effort. My deep appreciation goes to Wendell Castle and Lorry Parks, director of Wendell Castle, Inc., who have been extremely helpful in all the developmental phases of the exhibition and catalogue. Alexander F. Milliken also provided valuable assistance.

The exhibition was developed and organized by Davira S. Taragin, curator of twentieth-century decorative arts and design at the Detroit Institute of Arts. It was curated by Ms. Taragin and Edward S. Cooke, Jr., assistant curator of American decorative arts and sculpture at the Museum of Fine Arts, Boston. Special thanks are in order to Grant Holcomb, director of the Memorial Art Gallery at the University of Rochester, whose role in initiating this project was crucial to its success. Ms. Taragin, Mr. Cooke, and Joseph Giovannini are to be congratulated for their insightful contributions to the catalogue.

The efforts of various staff members at the Detroit Institute of Arts should also be acknowledged. Special gratitude is due Jennifer Way, who tirelessly researched material for the catalogue. Dirk Bakker, director of photography at the museum, is responsible for the outstanding color photographs of the artist's work. He was ably assisted by Robert Hensleigh, Timothy Thayer, and Francesca Quasarano. Cynthia Newman Helms edited the catalogue; her patience and careful attention to all its many facets are much appreciated. Julia Henshaw, director of museum publications, Julie Chickola, student intern, and Opal Hodge, secretary, also assisted with the preparation of the catalogue. Phyllis J. Browning, Deborah A. Moore, and Melanie Holcomb, all of the department of twentieth-century art, helped in numerous ways.

Other members of the staff who provided valuable assistance include Judith Dressel, head registrar, and Terry Segal, associate registrar; Barbara Heller, head conservator, Carol Forsythe, objects conservator, Matthew Fleischman, assistant objects conservator, and Valerie Dorge, Andrew W. Mellon fellow; Louis Gauci, group director of exhibitions and design, and Robert Loew, Jr., design and construction coordinator; Donald Jones, associate director of development, and Mary Piper, grants coordinator; Tara Robinson, associate curator of education; James Gibeau, audio-visual specialist, and Christopher Claypoole, music consultant; Lisa Steele, group director of marketing and public relations, and Margaret M. DeGrace, associate director of public relations.

At the participating museums, I would like to thank Janet Kardon, Director, American Craft Museum; Elizabeth Hawkes, associate curator, Delaware Art Museum; Susan Dodge Peters, assistant director for education, and Nancy Malone, assistant to the director, Memorial Art Gallery, University of Rochester; Frederick A. Brandt, curator, twentieth-century art, and Richard B. Woodward, manager of art services, Virginia Museum of Fine Arts.

Finally, I would like to express deep appreciation to the lenders who have so graciously agreed to share their works with the public through this exhibition, and to Steinway & Sons and Hammell Music, Inc., for their special efforts in making it possible to include the *500,000th Commemorative Steinway Piano and Bench* as part of the Detroit showing.

Samuel Sachs II
Director, Detroit Institute of Arts

Within the past few years, the maturation of the Studio Craft movement in America has created a strong need for scholarship in the field. Although recent publications and such exhibitions as "The Eloquent Object," organized by the Philbrook Museum of Art in Tulsa (1987), have begun to address the history of this movement, much work is still needed to document the careers of the leading artist-craftsmen as well as the numerous craft fairs, galleries, and exhibitions, many of them sponsored by university art galleries, that have provided exposure for these artists, and the patrons, both public and private, who have had the insight to support the work in spite of resistance from the art world. The history of the movement and its participants also needs to be critically examined within the larger context of twentieth-century art in order to document conclusively the important exchange of ideas that has occurred among contemporary painters, sculptors, architects, and craftsmen.

The idea for this exhibition developed directly from the realization that few scholarly studies have been done of the work of the leading contemporary artist-craftsmen associated with the Studio Craft movement. A lecture by Castle in 1986 at the Detroit Institute of Arts revealed that while various segments of his career had been explored in survey shows or small one-person exhibitions, the breadth of his experimentation with wood over the past thirty years had not been elucidated nor had the resulting body of work ever been seen in its entirety.

The essays in this book, which accompanies the first retrospective exhibition of Castle's work, attempt to place the evolution of Castle's oeuvre both within the context of the emerging Studio Craft movement and within the mainstream of American art in the 1960s and 1970s. It is hoped the issues addressed here will stimulate further scholarly research on this very exciting postwar movement as well as on Castle himself as one of the leaders of the art-furniture movement in America.

The authors wish to express their gratitude to the following persons and institutions whose assistance and support have been invaluable in the preparation of this book and the accompanying exhibition:

Ronald D. Abramson, Connie Ayres, Dr. and Mrs. Irwin R. Berman, Greg Bloomfield, Scott Burton, Graham Campbell, Alison Castle, John Cederquist, Barbara Cowles, John Dunnigan, Dr. and Mrs. Robert Fishman, Peggy Fleming, Dan Friedman, Richard Gallerani, Frank Gehry, Henry Geldzahler, Mr. and Mrs. George H. Hawks, Jr., Katherine Jannach Hinds, Penelope Hunter-Stiebel, Isabell Hurdle, Karen Boyd Johnson, Mr. and Mrs. Samuel C. Johnson, Peter T. Joseph, Nancy Jurs, Richard Kagan, Peter Klingensmith, Chris Lodermeier, Terry Lysogorski, Martin Z. Margulies, Mervin B. Martin, Alphonse Mattia, Gertrude Moore, Glorya Mueller, Lynn Mulinger, Fran Nelson, Richard Scott Newman, Albert Paley, Lorry Parks, Ronald Pearson, Christine Pittel, John Prip, Stephen Proctor, Max Protetch, Ruth Raible, Anton Rajer, Victor von Reventlow, Brian Rooney, Carol Saltwick, Jackie Schuman, Richard W. Sherin, William Sloane, Paul J. Smith, Rosanne Somerson, Donald Sottile, Richard M. Spinks, Wendy Stayman, William H. Straus, Naomi Vogelfanger, Jeff Webster, Don Williams, Marc A. Williams, Townsend Wolfe, Bernice Wollman, Mrs. Marvin Wurth, Robin Young, Myrna Ziff, Scott Zupp.

Rene Barilleaux, Madison Art Center; Katie Block, Harcus Gallery; William R. Boles, *Boston Globe*; Frederick A. Brandt, Virginia Museum of Fine Arts; Nancy Buckett, Oxford Gallery; Mark Burhans, The Dairy Barn, Southeastern Ohio Cultural Center; Anthony Urbane Chastain-Chapman, *Fine Woodworking*; Carol Craven, Alexander Johnston, and Alexander F. Milliken, Alexander F. Milliken, Inc.; Sherry Cromwell-Lacy, Kansas City Art Institute; Theresa Delemarre, Hood Museum of Art; Mary Denison, Maccabees Life Insurance Company; Harry Dennis, *American Ceramics*; Christine Droll, Oakland Museum; Dona Everson, Silvermine Guild Arts Center; Linda Foss and Jonathan Fairbanks, Museum of Fine Arts, Boston; Janet Farber, Joslyn Art Museum; Sue Farrell, *Rochester City Newspaper*; Barbara Fendrick, Fendrick Gallery; Russel Flinchum, Linda Seckelson, and Doris Stowens, American Craft Council; Saundra Goldman, DeCordova and Dana Museum and Park; Suzanne K. Gourlie, Library, Dayton Art Institute; Peggy Haney, Southeast-Missouri State University Museum; Judy Heinmann, Bevier Gallery, Rochester Institute of Technology; Anna Holcombe, Gallery at the State University of New York, Brockport; Katherine S. Howe, The Museum of Fine Arts, Houston; Tim Hoy, Hammell Music, Inc.; Peggy Itzen, *Austin American Statesman*; Karen Janoury, University of Nebraska, Lincoln; Bebe Pritam Johnson, Pritam and Eames Gallery; Katie Johnson, San Angelo Museum of Fine Arts; Rick Kaufmann, Art et Industrie; Don Keith, Gunlocke Company; Mary Knetchel, Niagara County Community College; Sandy LaRouche, Famous-Barr Company; Robin C. Lockbee, Northern Illinois University; Kate Lydon, The Society for Art in Crafts; Frank Mazurco, Steinway & Sons; Linda McCandless, *Finger Lakes Magazine*; Diane Mervis, *Syracuse Herald-Journal*; Gary Metzner, Hokin Kaufman Gallery, Inc.; Pat Myers, The Travelers Mortgage Services; Ellen Meyette, Renwick Gallery, Smithsonian Institution; R. Craig Miller, The Metropolitan Museum of Art; Nadine Moore, *Indianapolis Star*; Sally Morgan, Penland School; Milo M. Naeve, The Art Institute of Chicago; Cynthia Nalevanko, Lannan Foundation; Ron Netsky, *Rochester Democrat and Chronicle*; Lee Nordness, Lee Nordness Galleries, Inc.; Sharon Olson, Palo Alto Library; Cynthia Ott, Darcy Tell, and Jeanne Zanke, Archives of American Art, Smithsonian Institution; Bernard Pasqualini, Free Library, Philadelphia; Lany D. Perkins, Joe and Emily Lowe Art Gallery, Syracuse University; Margarete Roeder, Margarete Roeder Gallery and Editions, Inc.; Ann Rogel, The Worcester Center for Crafts; Don Scheid, University of Kansas; Ann Shimmon, Museum of Art, Rhode Island School of

Design; Ellen Simak, Hunter Museum of Art; Marilyn Stokstad, University of Kansas; Rick and Ruth Snyderman, Snyderman Gallery; Carl Solway, Carl Solway Gallery; Mark Spencer, Haggerty Museum, Marquette University; Richard M. Spinks, S. C. Johnson & Son, Inc.; Kevin Stayton and Celestina Ucciferri, The Brooklyn Museum; Jane Tesso, Case Western Reserve University; Betty Tinlot, Ten Arrow Gallery; Harish Trivedi, Library, *Dayton Daily News*; Rowena A. Van Hoof, The Fine Arts Museum of the South; Jan van der Marck, Detroit Institute of Arts; Maria Via, Memorial Art Gallery, University of Rochester; Bret Waller, J. Paul Getty Museum; Gini Wheeler, Joint Librarian, Gannett Newspapers; Roberta Williams, Louisville Visual Arts Center Association; Ross Young, Twentieth-Century Gallery, Toronto; Ralph Youngren, Smith, Hinchman and Grylls; Anthea Zonars, American Craft Museum.

Albright-Knox Art Gallery, *Ann Arbor News*, *Boston Herald*, Carnegie Museum of Art, Enoch Pratt Free Library, Everson Museum of Art, Helen Drutt Gallery, Ithaca College, J. B. Speed Art Museum, Laguna Gloria Art Museum, Marian Goodman Gallery, Oakland Museum, *Oakland Tribune*, Orlando Public Library, *Providence Journal*, The Public Library of Cincinnati and Hamilton County, St. Louis Art Museum, Wichita Art Museum, Wolfe Publications.

Davira S. Taragin
Curator, Twentieth-Century Decorative Arts
  and Design
Detroit Institute of Arts

Edward S. Cooke, Jr.
Assistant Curator, American Decorative
  Arts and Sculpture
Museum of Fine Arts, Boston

Plate 1
Library Sculpture, 1965
(checklist no. 8)

A major phenomenon affecting the way furniture is made and understood in the 1980s has been the Studio Craft movement. By the late 1950s some of the more innovative American craftsmen in all media had begun to push aside the previously accepted emphasis on traditional materials and function in the crafts. This change in attitude primarily resulted from the fact that craftsmen enrolled in university art departments and art schools during the post–World War II education boom were increasingly exposed to the same training as their counterparts in the "fine" arts. As craftsmen incorporated the conceptual concerns of contemporary painters and sculptors into their work, they moved away from both the emphasis on function and the reverential treatment of materials that had characterized both the crafts and mass-produced designs. They began instead to create individual pieces, some functional, some not, or limited-edition works, all produced in small studio environments.

By the 1970s and 1980s, this approach to the object, which had originated in the crafts, was appearing in the work of painters, sculptors, and even architects. Even less concerned than the studio craftsmen with the limitations imposed by function and technical considerations, the creators of art furniture come to the movement from many different directions. Artists as diverse in background as Scott Burton, Michael Graves, Lucas Samaras, Howard Ben Tré, Robert Wilson, and Stephen de Staebler have ventured into making furniture. Art furniture may be handmade by the artist, or it may be produced, according to the artist's plans, in an independent craft workshop.

These artists have brought to the field a variety of approaches, resulting in a shift away from the emphasis on wood that characterized the furniture made by woodworkers during the craft revival of the 1950s and 1960s. Today many craftsmen, artists, and designers have transcended the traditional reverence for wood without sacrificing sensitivity to color, surface, and texture and without rejecting the mastery of technique that determines strength, solidness, and fit. The artists involved in furniture making have, for the most part, retained a functional aspect in their works. Many contemporary pieces, while often whimsical, illusionistic, or flashy in the extreme, can nevertheless actually be used as chairs, music stands, desks, or whatever. In other works function is treated in more cerebral fashion as the functional form becomes a metaphor for larger artistic issues.

The trailblazer in the transformation of the artist from woodworker to furniture artist, in the move away from an absolute reverence for a single material to a deeper concern with concept and meaning, and in gaining acceptance for furniture as a medium that can transcend the narrow bounds of the craft world has been Wendell Castle. Because he has consistently challenged the traditional concept of wooden furniture, Castle has been a major catalyst in the emergence of the art-furniture movement over the past thirty years. Through his continuing awareness and response to current trends in industrial design and sculpture, he has continually provided new interpretations of traditional furniture forms, with the result that his work as a whole embodies the development of handcrafted furniture as a major art form.

EARLY INFLUENCES

As a youth growing up in Holton, Kansas, Castle displayed a natural predilection for drawing and making models. He wanted to attend art school, but his parents strongly

THE CAREER OF WENDELL CASTLE
Davira S. Taragin and
Edward S. Cooke, Jr.

opposed such romanticism. To allay their concerns, he initially undertook business-administration and engineering courses at Baker University in Baldwin City, Kansas. However, in 1953, on the advice of his professors, Castle transferred to the University of Kansas and enrolled in the design department. During Castle's student years (1953–61), Kansas had a well-respected design faculty that included such sculptors as Elden C. Tefft and Bernard "Poco" Frazier. The school also sponsored a nationally recognized annual juried designer-craftsman exhibition.

Castle's course of study at the university introduced him to the field of designed household goods at a time when American industrial designers such as Charles and Ray Eames, George Nelson, and others were enjoying international reputations. Castle took courses in architectural and industrial design, drawing, sculpture, and jewelry, a curriculum that brought him into contact with students of such diverse backgrounds as laser sculptor Rockne Krebs and jeweler Robert Ebendorf. In 1960 Castle took a brief leave from his studies to work on interiors for a proposed moon base for the Radiation Corporation of Orlando, Florida. Shortly thereafter he realized that he was not interested in a career of designing furniture for the trade and did not want a confining nine-to-five job. Having decided that he wanted to be a sculptor, Castle returned to the University of Kansas and finished the course work for a master's degree in 1961.[1]

No single department, professor, or travel experience proved to be the primary catalyst for Castle's development; instead, it was books and magazines. In contemporary art journals he eagerly followed the work of such sculptors as Isamu Noguchi, Jean Arp, Henry Moore, Barbara Hepworth, Alexander Calder, and particularly Leonard Baskin, who treated large, laminated blocks of wood as if they were slabs of marble, creating highly simplified forms with a strong sense of wholeness, structural solidity, and power. From his reading, Castle began to realize the potential of wood in the creation of monumental sculpture. But the ultimate source of inspiration for his work came from a book used in his industrial-design course: Don Wallance's *Shaping America's Products*.[2] Included in this book of case studies demonstrating the best new approaches in the integration of art and utility is information about the woodworkers George Nakashima and Wharton Esherick. Castle was so impressed with what he read that, during a trip to the East Coast in 1958, he visited the studios of both Calder and Esherick. While the renowned Calder spent considerable time with the young artist from Kansas, the reclusive Esherick refused to see him. In spite of this, and although he was impressed with the humor of Calder's work, Castle realized that there was a greater affinity between his concerns and those of the reclusive woodworker and immediately resolved to model himself after Esherick.

Philosophically, Esherick was the perfect mentor for Castle. Trained in a formal academic art program, Esherick had found a niche in the art world by making woodblock prints, sculpture, and sculptural furniture. Castle felt a spiritual rapport with Esherick as a sculptor who had turned to furniture as his medium of choice and who was neither pure craftsman nor pure designer. As Castle remarked just after Esherick's death in 1970, "Esherick taught me that the making of furniture could be a form of sculpture."[3]

Castle also felt a kinship with Esherick on aesthetic grounds. Esherick thought that most contemporary furniture lacked beauty and personality. He rebelled against the use of metal and the rectilinear construction typical of the International Style and other machine-age furniture and found the straightforward lines of post–World War II wooden furniture to be bland and predictable. As Esherick later stated his position: "I was impatient with the contemporary furniture being made—straight lines, sharp edges, and right angles—and I conceived free angles and free forms, making the edges of my tables flow so that they would be attractive to feel or caress. So I suppose it is called 'free form' furniture."[4] This view clearly foreshadows Castle's philosophy of the 1960s and 1970s.

Not only did Esherick's aesthetic influence Castle, so too did his choice of the technical means to execute it. Esherick possessed only basic skills in woodworking and abhorred the craftsman's obsession with tools, materials, and processes as ends unto themselves. He relied on simple joints such as post-and-rung construction, bridle joints (often simply nailed together), and through-tenons; for more complex pieces he often employed professional technicians to execute his ideas. Finding the actual woodworking tedious and frustrating, Esherick focused instead on the initial idea and the final shaping.

Simple techniques and a concern for sculpted form also characterized Castle's early work. Since Castle lacked formal training in furniture making, he used the most expedient means to achieve his ideas. For some works he relied on doweled-and-mitered construction, techniques better suited to frames than to furniture. When he used mortise-and-tenon joints, he cut his tenons on a band saw and his mortises with a drill and coping saw instead of using a table saw and mortising machine or a backsaw and mortising chisels.

EARLY WORKS (1959–63)

Castle's works from 1959 to 1963 can be divided into three categories: those that derive from his industrial-design studies, the Esherick-influenced pieces, and abstract figurative sculptures. Castle's earliest piece was based on his industrial-design studies. His first *Chair*, made in 1958–59 (pl. 2), is rooted in mid-1950s industrial-furniture design. The streamlined form combines the stance of George Nelson's seating pieces and the finned detailing of 1950s automobiles. The rake of the fins endows the chair with a profile similar to that of chairs designed by the Italian Gio Ponti, while the slightly arched stretchers are a trademark of mid-1950s Danish furniture, seen in the work of Jorgen Hoj and many others. The influence of Danish design was strong throughout the United States at that time, particularly at the School for American Craftsmen at the Rochester Institute of Technology where the Danish-trained Tage Frid was on the faculty. In fact, Rochester furniture craftsman Robert Donovan made a string-upholstered chair much like Castle's in 1959.[5]

A *Rocker* that Castle made in 1963 (pl. 3) evokes the lines and the feeling of motion of Le Corbusier's famous chaise longue. As the New York designer Vladimir Kagan had done in a rocker created seven years earlier, Castle translated Corbusier's tubular metal form into wood to soften its visual impact and to lessen its mechanistic quality.[6] Castle also challenged Le Corbusier's emphasis on undecorated structural form by introducing the date "1963" on a stretcher directly below the seat. The use of these numerals is the first example of Castle's interest in writing as imagery.

The conventions of contemporary industrial design are also evident in a 1962 *Chest of Drawers* (pl. 5). The rectangular drawer case recalls designs from the 1940s and early 1950s by such American designers as George Nelson, Charles and Ray Eames, and Edward J.

Plate 2
Chair, 1958–59
(checklist no. 1)

Plate 3
Rocker, 1963
(checklist no. 5)

19

Wormley, but Castle subtly shaped the boards of the carcass with a plane and mounted the drawers on branchlike, bent-laminated legs in an effort to have nature tame and contain the rectilinear design. This combination of rectilinear forms drawn from industrial design with curvilinear sculptural effects makes manifest the foundation of Castle's aesthetic.

Castle's most innovative works from this early period are those that follow Esherick's aesthetics. The asymmetry and concave planes with rounded edges found in Castle's *Stool Sculpture* of 1959 (pl. 4) relate generally to the linear abstract sculpture of the 1950s but more specifically to Esherick's sculptural work and furniture of the 1930s and 1940s (see fig. 1).[7] While the chair's mitered-and-doweled construction was simple, Castle devoted considerable time to the shaping and sanding of the parts. The use of ivory as an accent, a feature not found in the work of other American woodworkers at that time, foreshadowed his later interest in exotic materials as accents.

Castle's *Music Stand* of 1964 (pl. 6) is another piece that owes a great deal to his mentor. Esherick's *Music Stand* of 1960 (fig. 4), a framed rack with horizontal slats set on three gracefully curved legs, became an archetypal form for American woodworkers.[8] Castle's version incorporates an unframed rack and bent-laminated legs, which endow the form with a lighter, more graceful feeling. Castle later recalled that he had conceived his music rack as a treelike form: "The legs would be root-like, embracing the ground in a gentle, but regular, organic curve. From them, the trunk would ascend like a supple, bent sapling. A twig-like appendage would descend to hold the easel."[9]

Castle did not begin creating abstract sculptural forms until 1960. Over the next four years he intermittently worked on a series of laminated figurative sculptures. Initially, these works had softly rounded, textured bodies and faces joined together by elongated dowels. By 1962 he had abandoned the doweled forms to create handcarved works (see fig. 3) that are strongly reminiscent of the work of sculptor Leonard Baskin (see fig. 2) in their emphasis on the integrity of the block of wood. These sculptures are important within Castle's oeuvre primarily since they show his early concern with the human figure, a theme that reappears in his clocks in the mid-1980s.

CASTLE MOVES TO RIT AND TURNS TO LAMINATION

In mid-1961 Castle and his first wife, Joyce Malicky, an opera singer, moved to New York in hopes of advancing their careers. By that time the New York craft world had already begun to recognize Castle's work. In 1959 Florence Eastmead, executive director of America House, a major sales outlet for American craftsmen in New York City, had chosen Castle as one of two prizewinners for furniture in the highly regarded "Designer-Craftsman Exhibition" sponsored by the University of Kansas. His prizewinning entry, the walnut *Chair* of 1958–59 (pl. 2), was subsequently featured in the review of the exhibition in *Craft Horizons*, at that time the leading publication on contemporary crafts, which was published by the American Craftsmen's Council (now the American Craft Council).[10] It was his non-functional chairs, however, that catapulted him into the limelight. *Stool Sculpture* (pl. 4) was juried into the "Mid-America Exhibition" of 1960 at the Nelson Gallery-Atkins Museum in Kansas City, while the similar *Scribe's Stool*, 1962, received considerable press when it was exhibited in New York at the Museum of Contemporary Crafts as part of the "Young Americans" exhibition of 1962.[11]

Figure 1
Wharton Esherick, American, 1887–1970, *Oak Spiral Stair*, 1930, and *Side Stair*, 1940, in Esherick's studio. Paoli, Pennsylvania, The Wharton Esherick Museum.

Figure 2
Leonard Baskin, American, born 1922, *Oppressed Man*, 1960. New York, Whitney Museum of American Art, Purchase (60.30).

Figure 3
Wendell Castle, *Hand*, ca. 1962.

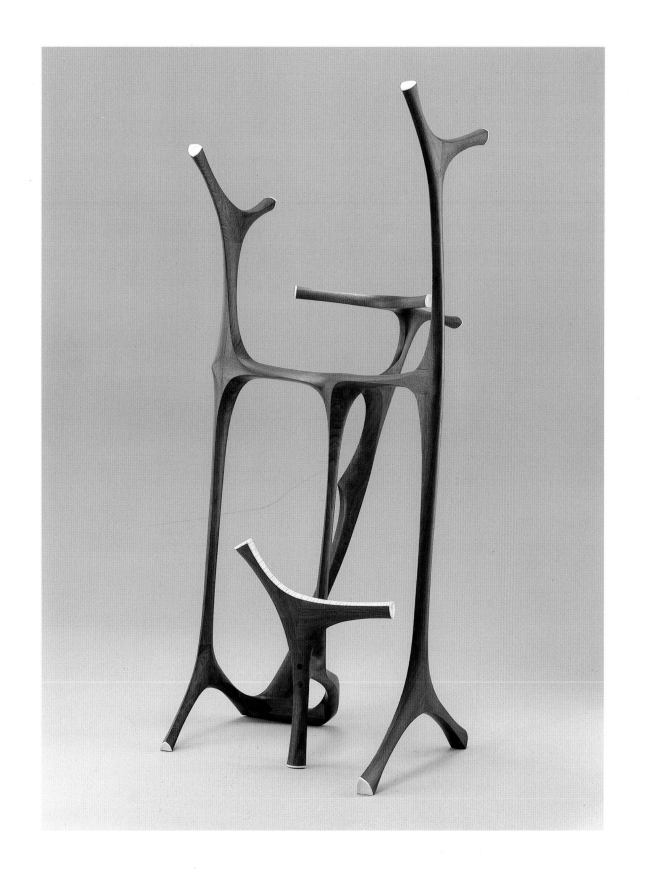

Plate 4
Stool Sculpture, 1959
(checklist no. 2)

21

Plate 5
Chest of Drawers, 1962, two views
(checklist no. 3)

Castle's success in the "Young Americans" show had an immediate impact on his career. Perhaps the most important result was his move to Rochester, New York, to assume a teaching position at the Rochester Institute of Technology. At about this time, impressed by the critical attention accorded to the sculptural, biomorphic works of Frans Wildenhain, the ceramics instructor at RIT, Harold Brennan, RIT's dean of fine and applied arts, realized that the craft world was undergoing a dramatic transformation. It was clear to Brennan that the distinction between craft and fine art had begun to blur as an emphasis on conceptual issues and innovative techniques replaced a reliance on traditional techniques and materials.

Brennan considered Wildenhain the ideal department head and began to look for individuals of comparable approach to craft to head RIT's other departments. With this in mind, Brennan contacted Paul J. Smith, then assistant to the president of the American Craftsmen's Council, and asked who the best sculptural furniture maker was at that time. Based on what he had seen at the "Young Americans" exhibition, Smith recommended Castle. Castle accepted the position at RIT and began work in the fall of 1962, with William Keyser, a student of Tage Frid, the former department head, as his associate. Wildenhain acknowledged Castle's presence in Rochester with a one-person show in November of that year at Shop One, a local artists' cooperative owned by Wildenhain and metalworker Ronald Pearson, among others.[12]

RIT provided an environment in which Castle could develop a new style. Because students were allowed to use the woodshop only from nine to five on weekdays, Castle had exclusive access to the space at night and on weekends. The woodshop was an ideal space, providing a full range of power equipment, including jointers, surface planers, band saws, and clamps. Castle also benefited from observing the technical competence of Keyser, who was well versed in joinery and construction. The combination of the availability of more machines and exposure to some sophisticated joinery allowed Castle to expand greatly his technical repertoire and design sense.

Having added more technical means to his Esherick-influenced aesthetic sensibilities, Castle sought to break away from the traditional world of rectilinear furniture executed in styles that echoed the past. Instead he sought a more expressive, ahistorical, and organic approach to furniture. As Castle later wrote:

> I believe that furniture should not be derived from furniture. This practice can only lead to variations on existing themes. New concepts will arise only when we clear our minds of preconceived notions about the way furniture should look. Most important is the notion that these ideas must be conceived with vision. To me an organic form has the most exciting possibilities. An organic form is not so clearly understood in one glance. My forms may be plant-like, shell-like, human-like, animal-like, or bone-like, all at once or in various combinations. I make no attempt to reconstruct or stylize natural forms, but I try rather to produce a synthesis or metamorphosis of natural forms.[13]

To execute his vision, Castle rejected the standard construction techniques then in vogue and instead relied on the techniques of large wooden sculpture, specifically lamination. From the duck decoys and figurative sculptures of the nineteenth century (and from contemporary abstract sculpture) and the balsa-wood airplane models of his youth, Castle

Figure 4
Wharton Esherick, *Music Stand*, 1960. Paoli, Pennsylvania, The Wharton Esherick Museum.

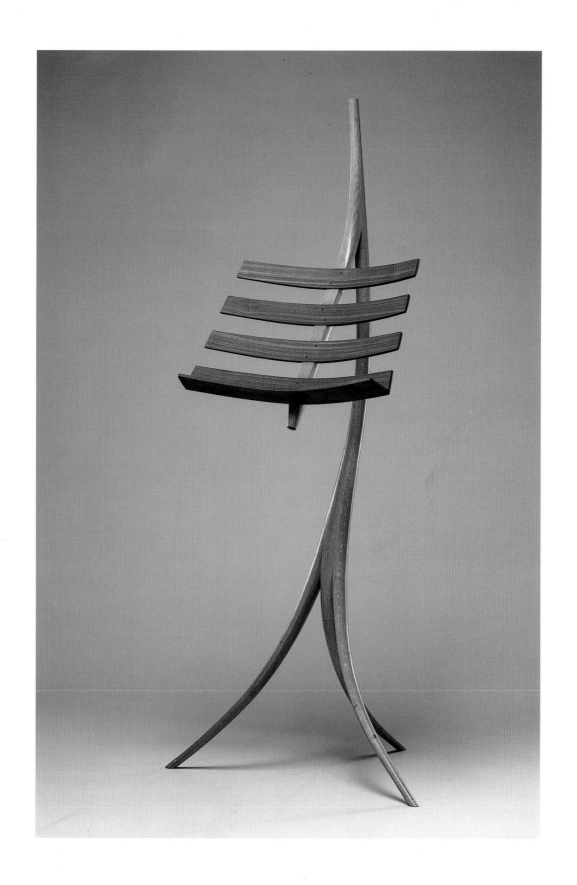

Plate 6
Music Stand, 1964
(checklist no. 6)

borrowed the technique of stack lamination, in which boards are glued together to form a mass that is then carved into shape. Castle devised a variation of this technique in which the boards were preshaped to follow the general outline of the final form. To do this, he had to visualize the desired form as a series of cross sections and then make careful dimensional calculations so that the necessary boards could be cut to fit very closely the general contours of the piece. He first band-sawed one-inch boards to follow the general contours of the piece and then band-sawed out the inside of each board. The latter step permitted him to lighten the weight of the final piece. With the various layers of the form properly shaped, Castle began to glue and clamp them together, layer by layer. Once the form was complete, Castle dragged a chain saw along the outside edges. Additional smoothing and shaping was done with a power planer, a pneumatic ball mill or chisel, and a body grinder. The final series of tools included chisels and gouges, scrapers, and sandpaper. Although lamination was frequently used by contemporary sculptors in the 1950s, Castle was definitely the first artist-craftsman to use it on a regular basis over an extended period of time in furniture construction. As Castle proudly stated, such techniques were "rarely" associated with furniture.[14]

From Poco Frazier, Castle had learned bent lamination, a technique in which a board was sawn into thin strips that were then glued together and clamped against a curved pattern to produce a slender, but strong, curved form. This technique "reprogrammed" the structural "memory" of the board to ensure maximum tensile strength without bulky amounts of wood. While sculptors employed this technique to build appendages and tight curves, Castle applied it to the legs of furniture. Perhaps his most notable use of this technique is found in the *Music Stand* of 1964 (pl. 6) (first version 1963). The shop at RIT facilitated these techniques: the jointers and planers permitted exact surface preparation, thereby ensuring a neat, tight glue joint; and the large space and the wide selection of clamps eased the glue-up of pieces.

After arriving at RIT, Castle quickly increased his technical repertoire. But, while he mastered dovetails and table-sawed mortise-and-tenon joints, he never overemphasized the means at the expense of the final result. As Castle has stated: "Who cares what tools were used? If you have been able to push the material beyond its normal form, fine."[15] Unlike other woodworkers of the period who emphasized their technical skill by using joints, such as dovetails and wedged-through tenons, as decorative features, Castle viewed joinery as simply part of the process.

CASTLE DEVELOPS HIS SCULPTURAL APPROACH

During his early years at RIT, Castle continued to eschew historical precedents and traditional forms, seeking instead to create original sculptural works. His cherry *Blanket Chest* of 1963 (pl. 8) resembles a chest only in that it functions as a container. Aesthetically, with its large, rounded cavity resting on a short, narrow base, it is reminiscent of the small figurative doweled sculptures that Castle had worked on between 1960 and 1961. It lacks the dovetailed or rabbeted-and-nailed carcass construction of traditional chests. Rather than framing-in a cavity using those techniques, Castle created the interior by hollowing out his stacked boards. The top was also carved out of the solid mass rather than being of board-

Plate 7
Desk, 1967
(checklist no. 10)

Plate 8
Blanket Chest, 1963, two views
(checklist no. 4)

and-batten or framed-panel construction, the two more common techniques for constructing the lids of boxes or containers.

Similarly, in a *Desk* of 1967 (pl. 7), which he sold to the Johnson Collection of Contemporary Crafts for the "Objects USA" exhibition of 1969, Castle broke with the traditional rules of furniture design. Eschewing a carcass construction of skirt panels tenoned into vertical legs or vertical legs tenoned into a dovetailed case, Castle used scarf lamination to build the serpentine base and stack lamination for the writing surface, which he then embellished with silver leaf. As in the *Blanket Chest*, Castle accommodated function but placed greater emphasis on the work's organic shape.

For Castle the base of a table or desk is an essential design element. It is the factor that determines whether a piece of furniture transcends its function and becomes a sculpture. As Castle explained:

> I kind of like the thing underneath the most. I was interested in . . . getting the base out from under the table and making the whole thing a piece of sculpture. I've done quite a few pieces where the base lays along the floor and comes up at appropriate times to hold something but yet becomes a very important design element in itself, as important as the top, not separated from the top.[16]

Castle equated his work with that of such sculptors as the Englishman Anthony Caro because they too had rejected the separation of the base from the form.

In other work from the mid-1960s the joinery is a bit more evident. A *Bookcase* made in 1967 (pl. 9) is dovetailed together but the joints are relatively unobtrusive, the laminated swelling of the proper right side being the dominant visual element. Although bentwood technologies existed that would have allowed him to make this side out of continuous boards and were used by him elsewhere, Castle chose the easier technique of stack lamination even though this resulted in unsightly lines and patches on the surface.

A *Desk* of 1965 (pl. 10) followed the basic form of traditional desks more closely than did the silver-leaf–topped example, but the method of building this form was distinctly Castle's. The basic design recalls Germanic desks of the late eighteenth century, especially the work of David Roentgen (see fig. 5), but Castle constructed it with laminated legs doweled into a stack-laminated horizontal element. Instead of sliding dovetailed drawers, he incorporated storage compartments with hinged lids on either side of the writing surface. In contrast to the desk, the accompanying chair demonstrates a greater interest in traditional construction and a continued reliance on industrial design. The use of bent lamination to form the three legs and of through-tenons to secure the seat to the legs linked this work to the woodworking mainstream at RIT.

Castle's development in the mid- to late 1960s was strongly influenced by the work of the American sculptor George Sugarman (see fig. 6). He saw an affinity between his own work and the large, sprawling, polychromatic, laminated-wood floor sculptures Sugarman was doing at the time. Castle not only admired Sugarman's daring in denying the sensuousness of the medium by painting his works, but also applauded Sugarman's ability to create strong sculptural statements through the juxtaposition of a series of dissimilar forms that unfolded in a continuous sequence in space.

Figure 5
David Roentgen, German, 1734–1807, *Desk*, 18th century. Nuremberg, Germanisches Nationalmuseum.

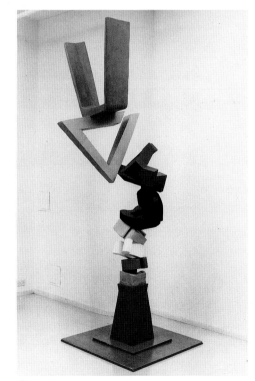

Figure 6
George Sugarman, American, born 1912, *C-Change*, 1964. Courtesy of the Robert Miller Gallery, New York.

Plate 9
Bookcase, 1967
(checklist no. 9)

Plate 10
Desk and Chair, 1965, two views
(checklist no. 7)

Like Sugarman, on whom he wrote for *Craft Horizons*,[17] Castle viewed medium and technique only as the means to a sculptural end. He valued topographical contouring, ridged transitions, and fantastic shapes much more highly than practical purpose or function. Castle developed three different conceptual formulas: a sculptured base from which the form grew up or down, a small base anchored to the floor to which were joined many units, and a form fastened to the wall or ceiling. Many of these forms proved problematic as functional furniture. For example, the creation in the late 1960s of a *Dining Table* (fig. 7) for the Douglas Bakers of Rochester resulted in disaster. Hung from the ceiling, the table lacked the necessary strength at the junctures of the arms with the ceiling and with the table surface. When it began to develop serious cracks, Castle was fearful that it might crash upon itself so he removed it. In other cases, the considerable stress placed upon glued joints—in his early works Castle used common white glue rather than stronger adhesives in order to avoid telltale glue lines—often led to delaminated pieces that had to be reglued and restacked.

The comfort and security of his academic job allowed Castle to begin taking commissioned work. In 1964 the Gleason Company of Rochester commissioned him to make a suite of office furniture for ten thousand dollars. With the profits from this job, about six thousand dollars, Castle purchased a complete set of his own machinery—band saw, table saw, planer, jointer, drill press, sander, and clamps—and at the end of that year leased a carriage house near RIT. He also hired an RIT student as a full-time assistant for the summer months and in 1966 hired Richard Scott Newman, a woodworker and musical instrument maker, as his first year-round assistant. He used his employees in the preparation of stock—surfacing boards and sawing according to his cross-section drawings—and in the tedious final scraping and sanding.

Figure 7
Wendell Castle, *Dining Table, Chairs, and Light*, 1966, for the residence of the Douglas Bakers, Rochester, New York.

CASTLE'S REPUTATION GROWS

From the beginning Castle displayed strong business acumen. Rather than concentrating on gallery sales, he focused on getting his works placed in shows that would increase his visibility and enhance his reputation, assuming commissions would follow. In 1965 Castle won first prize in the annual "Rochester–Finger Lakes Exhibition," sponsored by the University of Rochester's Memorial Art Gallery, and as a result was accorded his first one-person museum exhibition, an event that proved critical for his career. The exhibition, at the Memorial Art Gallery in 1965, drew record attendance and served to acquaint the local community with his work, resulting in important sales and commissions and the beginnings of several long-term artist-patron relationships.[18]

Like all the museum exhibitions in which he was to participate, this show was important for Castle's aesthetic growth because it gave him the opportunity to realize ideas that were too avant-garde for his routine commissioned work. The exhibition enabled him to expand his range beyond the design and creation of individual pieces of furniture. Once again, Esherick was Castle's inspiration. Castle acknowledges that the older artist taught him the importance of the entire sculptural environment, an approach that is well demonstrated in Esherick's own home and studio. *Library Sculpture* (pl. 1), created specifically for the Memorial Art Gallery exhibition, was Castle's first attempt at creating a suite of furniture for a specific space. Consisting of a writing desk, three seating elements, and a light fixture, it also represents Castle's first attempt to integrate several different functions into one cohesive, utilitarian unit, thus eliminating the necessity of mixing styles and, in his own words, "putting one piece of furniture on another."[19]

During this time Castle's work began to figure prominently in national and international craft exhibitions, especially those organized by the American Craftsmen's Council. Although few woodworkers were recognized by the council and woodworking ranked low in the craft hierarchy, far below ceramics, fiber, and metal, Castle's furniture appeared in survey shows at small museums and university art galleries such as the Worcester Art Museum (Massachusetts), the Addison Gallery of American Art (Phillips Academy, Andover, Massachusetts), and the Krannert Art Museum (University of Illinois, Champaign), as well as in regional competitions such as the one organized at the Delaware Art Museum by the American Craftsmen's Council. His *Music Stand* (pl. 6) was included in the exhibition of American crafts that Jack Lenor Larsen organized for the Thirteenth Triennale (1964) in Milan. A grant from the American Craftsmen's Council enabled the School for American Craftsmen to produce a documentary film about the design and manufacture of this piece. Similarly, Castle was one of several craftsmen chosen to represent the United States at the 1966 "Internationales Kunsthandwerk" exhibition in Stuttgart, which at the time was considered the most significant craft exhibition in Europe.[20]

The strongest indication of Castle's growing position in the craft world was his inclusion in the 1964 exhibition "The American Craftsman," at the Museum of Contemporary Crafts in New York, which was organized to coincide with the New York World's Fair of that year. Among the thirty distinguished American craftsmen included in this show, Castle was one of only three woodworkers. Paul J. Smith, curator of the show, juxtaposed Castle's work with that of Sam Maloof and Esherick to demonstrate the wide variety of approaches that existed in contemporary woodworking. Smith was so taken with Castle's work that less than two years later he included him in the internationally acclaimed five-person show "Fantasy Furniture," also at the Museum of Contemporary Crafts. Particularly significant for Castle's career was the considerable press coverage his works received, including a review in *Art in America*.[21] During this period Castle continued to sell his work through America House in New York. Income from sales enabled him, in 1967, to hire more assistants.

This phase of Castle's career reached a climax in 1966 when he met Lee Nordness, a New York dealer. Although Nordness had focused on showing contemporary figurative painting and sculpture since opening his gallery in 1958, he had also been involved with the emerging contemporary craft world since the mid-1960s. After seeing Castle's work in the Museum of Contemporary Crafts' 1962 "Young Americans" show, Nordness was tempted to ask Castle to join the gallery, but he had doubts about how the rest of his roster might feel if furniture were to be placed beside their paintings and sculptures. Shortly thereafter, while on a trip to the Midwest, Nordness was again impressed when he saw Castle's work exhibited at the University of Illinois. In 1966, having viewed the "Fantasy Furniture" show, he found that he agreed with Paul Smith that there was no other furniture maker as adventurous as Castle and without further hesitation undertook the promotion of Castle's work in New York. He purchased *Chest of Drawers* (pl. 5), which had been included in "Fantasy Furniture," and commissioned Castle to create a living-room suite for his penthouse apartment (the suite was later acquired by the Art Institute of Chicago), with the intention of using the commission to introduce his clients to Castle's work.

In 1968 Nordness decided to offer Castle the first one-person exhibition he had ever given to an artist-craftsman in his gallery. Indeed, Nordness claimed at the time that this show would "be the first time . . . a fine arts gallery has given an American artist/craftsman a one-man show."[22] Although the large laminated and shaped furniture sold only modestly, critical reaction was positive, with coverage in such magazines and newspapers as *Newsweek*, the *New York Times*, and the highly respected *Arts Magazine*.[23] The success of Castle's first exhibition led Nordness to bring fourteen other American craftsmen into his stable.[24]

In 1967 Nordness, with Smith as a consultant, had begun to work on building a major crafts collection for S. C. Johnson & Son, Inc., in Racine, Wisconsin. This effort resulted in 1969 in the landmark traveling exhibition and publication "Objects USA." For the next few years, at the same time as he worked on this seminal show and its catalogue, Nordness actively promoted Castle's career, using highly innovative and creative marketing approaches. One of his most imaginative advertisements, which appeared in *Art in America*, juxtaposed a photograph of the sofa that Castle had created for Nordness's own apartment with a bronze sculpture by the American artist David Aronson. The copy read: "Dare a sculpture endorse a sofa? Yes, when the sofa is created by one of the new breed of craftsmen-cum-artists."[25] This aggressive marketing, however, proved to be only moderately successful. In addition to working with department stores and home-furnishing centers, such as Gimbels, Abraham & Straus, and Sachs Quality Stores, in organizing small displays of crafts by Castle and other American craftsmen,[26] he successfully organized a one-person show of Castle's work that traveled to three midwestern museums.[27] During this time Nordness also was responsible for convincing patrons Samuel C. Johnson (of S. C. Johnson & Son, Inc.) and R. Philip Hanes, Jr. (of Hanes Dye and Finishing Company), to give Castle major commissions.[28]

THE EXPLORATION OF OTHER MEDIA AND
A MOVE AWAY FROM FUNCTION

Perhaps as a result of the growing national recognition he was receiving from the fine-arts community, Castle was increasingly uncomfortable with his close association with the craft world. In an effort to change this situation, in the late 1960s he modified certain elements of his aesthetic, moving away from the heaviness of form, the dark tonality of the wood, and the strong utilitarian nature that had typified his works.

Inspired by the painted laminated sculpture of George Sugarman, Castle began to paint his work as early as 1968.[29] Unfortunately, he found that the wood continued to expand and contract, cracking the paint. To remedy this, he stacked plywood, then covered the form with Fiberglas to reduce the amount of movement, and finally painted it. This construction proved better but still not satisfactory. In 1969 he made several pieces of handbuilt furniture out of what he refers to as "reinforced plastic," consisting of Styrofoam and metal stovepipe cores that he covered with Fiberglas putty and then painted.[30]

The changes in Castle's aesthetic coincided with his purchase in 1968 of an old soybean mill in Scottsville, New York, just southwest of Rochester. In this two-story wood-frame mill, Castle established both living and work space. The new studio, into which he moved in 1969, gave him more room and thus allowed greater flexibility in his choice of techniques, but it also removed him from the RIT community.

At the same time as he began exploring other media, Castle became dissatisfied with his teaching position at RIT. When students complained about the conflicting orientations of Castle and William Keyser and about Castle's overemphasis on his own work, Brennan tried to reorganize the department, placing Keyser in charge of the first two years of the curriculum and Castle in charge of the last two. Even this plan did not seem to help, and Castle's frustration mounted. Then James Krenov took over Keyser's position for the academic year 1969–70. Although Castle and Krenov began on an amiable footing, their fundamental differences soon became apparent.[31] Krenov's dogmatic emphasis on refined cabinetmaking techniques and his Scandinavian designs were unpalatable to Castle, and in 1970 he accepted a position as chairman of the sculpture department at the State University of New York at Brockport.

In his second one-person exhibition at the Lee Nordness Galleries in the spring of 1970, Castle again used a nonwood medium. The nine lamps that made up the show were of glass-reinforced polyester colored with shiny automobile enamel and finished with automobile lacquer. In an attempt to identify these works as sculpture, Castle gave each lamp a name; he has throughout his career continued this practice of naming his sculptural work. Of the nine lamps, *Benny* (pl. 11) is the most interesting because it was in this work that Castle first used neon, then a popular material in contemporary sculpture. Unlike such contemporary artists as Bruce Nauman and Chryssa, who were employing neon as the exclusive medium in their abstract sculptures, Castle used it simply as a decorative element, to frame and therefore emphasize the lines of the reinforced polyester form. The lamps were unlike any of Castle's previous work, and Nordness did not know how to respond:

> Needless to say, we didn't know it was going to be a lamp show until two weeks before the exhibition. . . . And of course this exhibition should have been slanted to appeal to a whole different kind of cliental [*sic*] of magazine people and trendsetters than the ones we aimed at, thinking, first it was a furniture exhibit and then realizing it was a lamp show. These are incidentally sculptures which happen to light.[32]

Nordness's reaction no doubt pleased Castle as he tried, even in his stack-laminated work of the period, to break away from his established reputation as a furniture craftsman. *Wall Table No. 16*, executed in 1969 (pl. 12), was Castle's first stack-laminated work in which the functional aspect is nearly nonexistent. With its diminutive tabletop and elongated legs that gracefully join the floor, tabletop, and wall, the sculpture calls into question the traditional position and function of a table's legs and top.

ENVIRONMENTAL WORKS

During the next two years Castle expanded his horizons to include the design of several buildings and environments. He designed the exterior of a large outdoor gazebo for the Douglas Bakers (pl. 13),[33] for whom he had earlier designed the hanging dining table; a laminated walnut spiral stair for the home of Samuel C. Johnson in Racine, Wisconsin;[34]

Plate 11
Benny, 1969
(checklist no. 11)

38

Plate 12
Wall Table No. 16, 1969
(checklist no. 12)

and a prototype for a full-sized Fiberglas house. A fourth large-scale project—the environment that Castle created for the 1970 "Contemplation Environments" exhibition at the Museum of Contemporary Crafts—attracted the most national attention. For this show Castle designed a womblike stack-laminated oak chamber with a flocked Fiberglas arched appendage (fig. 8). When a person climbed into the laminated chamber and closed the door, a light bulb located on the arched form turned on to indicate that the small room was in use. Castle used his knowledge of boat and car design in creating the upholstery in the interior as well as in determining the position of the seat, reading lamp, and skylight.[35] Since the Museum of Contemporary Crafts' exhibition coincided with the showing at the Museum of Modern Art of "Spaces," a series of gallery installations by six conceptual artists, the two shows were subject to comparison. However, it was felt that the works shown at MoMA were more intellectually sophisticated in their attempts to define and delimit space.[36]

In 1972–73 the City of Rochester finally granted its longtime resident the kind of recognition he desired and gave him a commission for a large outdoor sculpture. The resulting twelve-foot sculpture, *Twist* (fig. 9), with its interlocking forms that also serve as public seating, was the culmination of his three-year-long experimentation with glass-reinforced polyester.

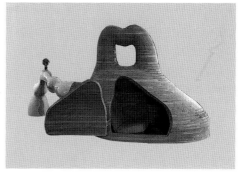

Figure 8
Wendell Castle, laminated oak chamber (in progress). Exhibited in "Contemplation Environments," Museum of Contemporary Crafts, New York, 1970.

Figure 9
Wendell Castle, *Twist*, 1972–73. Genesee Crossroads Park East, Rochester, New York.

opposite page
Plate 13
Gazebo, early 1970s
for the residence of the Douglas Bakers, Rochester, New York

PRODUCTION AND LIMITED-EDITION DESIGNS

During the early 1970s, because of his underlying interest in making his designs available to a wider audience, Castle began to design prototypes for a line of production furniture. Plastic was an ideal medium to begin this venture since the organic shapes of his designs were easily transferred into this material in its fluid stage. Through such magazines as *Domus*, Castle had followed the rise of Italian postwar design and its contributions to plastic furnishings, particularly noting the work of Joe Colombo and Ettore Sottsass. Castle made a series of prototypes of stack-laminated wood and putty filler for a *Molar Chair* (pl. 14), for another piece called simply the *Castle Chair*, and for an occasional table titled *Cookie Cutter*. He arranged for the fabrication of molds from these prototypes and for the production and distribution of the furniture to be undertaken by Stendig and Beylerian Limited. The artist's increasing emphasis on creating plastic furniture on contract led to the establishment of Wendell Castle Associates in 1970.[37]

According to Castle, the molar was "a more personal and unique sculptural form than usual[ly found] in fiberglass or reinforced plastic."[38] Castle's interest in the molar form may have resulted from his reading. In the 1930s several of the Surrealists were involved in making furniture with humanistic qualities that added a metaphorical dimension to utilitarian objects. The most publicized example of this furniture was Salvador Dali's design for a lip-shaped settee, which was produced by Jean-Michel Frank. In the 1960s the Italian designers of Studio 65 responded to the Surrealist's precedent with the similarly shaped *Marilyn Love Seat*, manufactured by Gufram. Castle was also no doubt aware of the work of Italian Pop Art designers who created plastic furnishings that mimicked such mundane objects as giant boulders.[39]

The molar form no doubt appealed to Castle because the curvilinearity of the upper ridges of a tooth are similar to the organic shapes he had been exploring in his stack-laminated furniture. He was so interested in the motif that he designed an entire line around it, consisting of an armchair, dining chair, oval dining table, round dining table, settee, coffee table, shelf, child's chair, and floor lamp. Since Castle considered the line to be sculpture as well as functional furniture, he gave titles to several designs within the grouping; for instance, the child's chair was called *Baby Molar*, the shelf *Cloud Shelf*.

Although Castle had formed Wendell Castle Associates primarily to develop the plastic production lines, he also offered, like many other American craftsmen, limited "signed editions" of his familiar laminated forms, including music stands, two-seaters, desks and tables, and several lines of chairs.[40]

The *Two-Seater* of 1979 (pl. 15), purchased by the Museum of Fine Arts, Boston, for its gallery seating program,[41] was a form first introduced in 1973. The popularity of this design stemmed from the considerable publicity it had received in the mid-1970s. Versions of the settee had been included in several exhibitions in both Canada and the United States before the Metropolitan Museum of Art, New York, acquired a similar two-seater settee in 1977. When Penelope Hunter-Stiebel, then associate curator at the Metropolitan, installed the settee for the first time in the museum's twentieth-century decorative-arts galleries, it attracted the attention of John Russell of the *New York Times*, who lauded it above all the other contemporary crafts on view.[42] Hunter-Stiebel also featured it prominently in the Metropolitan's *Bulletin* on twentieth-century decorative arts,[43] thereby bringing Castle to

Figure 14
Wendell Castle, *Stair*, 1976, for Gannett
Headquarters, Rochester, New York.

There were woodworkers, however, who rejected lamination. Some of Castle's students, such as Jon Brooks and Howard Werner, were influenced by his sculptural approach and emphasis upon organic style, but to achieve these ends they eschewed lamination and instead developed subtractive techniques with which they fashioned furniture from large trees and stumps. Other furniture makers, such as Tage Frid, Jere Osgood, and Dan Jackson, questioned the soundness of stack-laminated furniture construction and instead emphasized the need for appropriate techniques such as traditional joints and newer forms of lamination, i.e., tapered or stave. But even for this group Castle provided an important reference point: their work became freer in light of his interest in concept and imagery, and they were galvanized into renewed efforts on behalf of traditional methods in response to his lack of respect for technique.

CASTLE MOVES AWAY FROM LAMINATION

Although Castle's production line continued through the 1970s, he grew dissatisfied with lamination. Bothered partly by the composite surface created by the lamination technique and partly by the increasing number of imitators, he sought to change direction. One catalyst for this change may have been the metalsmith Albert Paley, who moved to Rochester in 1969 to join the faculty at RIT. Paley's curvilinear aesthetic, which was similar to Castle's own, was strongly influenced by the jewelry of René Lalique and by the designs of the turn-of-the-century Spanish architect Antoni Gaudí. Paley's historical inclinations may have awakened in Castle a keen interest in the decorative arts and furniture of the past. At the same time Castle became more aware of others working in the field of handcrafted furniture. His inclusion in "Woodenworks," the 1972 exhibition at the Renwick Gallery in Washington, D.C., that focused attention on five contemporary furniture makers and reached a broad audience, caused Castle to reflect on his position in the movement. As he compared himself with Sam Maloof, George Nakashima, and Arthur Espenet Carpenter, Castle realized that he was aesthetically isolated from the movement's mainstream and that this may have put him at an economic disadvantage. As a result, Castle reassessed his extreme commitment to sculptural furniture and began to explore more fully the possibilities of furniture executed with highly sophisticated techniques, shifting his emphasis from form as art to workmanship as art.

This philosophical and artistic change is also manifested in Castle's changing relationship with John Makepeace, the dean of studio furniture making in England. Castle has said that when he first met Makepeace in 1970, he found the Englishman's attention to wood usage, fastidious joinery, and perfect finish to be silly. But by 1973 Castle had come to appreciate Makepeace's designs and workmanship. He was also envious of the highly skilled technicians who worked with Makepeace and allowed him to spend more time designing, increasing the shop's ability to produce sophisticated work. Wishing to devote more time to furniture design and to attempt more technically refined work, Castle asked Makepeace to find a skilled English technician who would follow Castle's designs. Makepeace recruited Stephen Proctor, who arrived in 1975 for a two-year trial period as Castle's shop foreman. Trained at the Royal College of Art in London, Proctor possessed excellent cabinetmaking skills and had a keen interest in innovative design. The workshop

Plate 17
Stair, 1980–81,
for the residence of Martin Z. Margulies,
Coconut Grove, Florida

benefited further by the addition in 1974 of Silas Kopf, an apprentice with a background in architecture, and Donald Sottile, a skilled woodworker, in 1977.

Castle's custom pieces, which he worked on at the same time as he worked on his production line, underwent a dramatic change in 1974. In that year he produced the first pinwheel gaming table, a form he continued to make with slight variations for the rest of the decade. There were several consistent components in this series: a top surface with a highly figured veneer panel in the middle; framing rails around this panel, each of which ended in a projection that was connected to the top of a leg with a double-pinned dovetail joint; and a tapering leg with a slight kick-out at the bottom. Rather than being made of oak, cherry, or walnut, the predominant woods in his earlier work, the veneered panels were of exotic or highly figured woods such as bubinga, zebrawood, and burled walnut. Only the shaped rails recalled his earlier laminated work. Castle first showed a pinwheel table with a set of his *Zephyr* production chairs at the 1975 "Language of Wood" exhibition at the State University of New York at Buffalo. The early gaming tables had square tops, and later ones were three-sided desk/tables with bowed edges, a shape derived from Esherick's work in the 1960s.[48] This more traditional type of furniture attracted considerable attention. The maple, zebrawood, and walnut example illustrated (pl. 18) was shown in the 1979 exhibition at the American Craft Museum, "New Handmade Furniture: American Furniture Makers Working in Hardwood," and in 1982 was purchased by the Brooklyn Museum.

52

Plate 18
Desk, 1977
(checklist no. 15)

ILLUSIONISTIC WORKS

In 1976 Castle's work took yet another developmental direction, one that combined his previous sculptural interest and his newer conventional orientation. While teaching sculpture at the State University of New York at Brockport, Castle assigned his students the exercise of drawing a coat hanging on a chair. Struck by the folds and the texture of the coat, Castle was intrigued by the idea of translating everyday objects into illusionistic wooden sculpture. This idea was reinforced while he was working on the design for the newel post of the Gannett staircase. Proctor suggested that Castle carve a cowboy hat, like the one he wore while working, on the top of the post. Castle decided against this, but his interest in realistic sculpture grew. His first attempt was a hat on a shelf. Recognizing that faultless carving was necessary to make the still life convincing, Castle hired an academically trained French carver. In 1978 the carver executed several works, including *Table with Hat and Scarf*, to instruct Castle, Proctor, and Sottile in the fine points of carving. Castle's ability to match his ideas with the personal strengths of his staff and his willingness to get short-term outside help when necessary (once Castle and Sottile became accomplished, the carver was let go) distinguishes his approach from this point on.

Over the next few years Castle created two different types of illusionistic objects: works like *Coatrack with Trench Coat*, 1978 (pl. 19), which used stack-laminated furniture forms, and those such as *Chair with Sport Coat*, 1978 (pl. 20), in which the furniture forms are traditionally constructed. The latter works manifest Castle's interest in the proper and accurate staging of his carved everyday objects. In the spirit of historicism occasioned by the American Bicentennial, Castle turned to Early American furniture forms such as William and Mary tables, Chippendale chairs and tables, and Federal tables. He built works based on these historical forms with appropriate traditional joinery, relying on lamination only to achieve the mass of the carved objects.

When Castle began creating these trompe l'oeil sculptures, contemporary American sculptors had already been exploring two- and three-dimensional illusionism for several years. Indeed, illusionism had been well received in the art market since the late 1960s. By the late 1970s two types of illusionism were in vogue. Either the object was reproduced so exactly as to appear real, as in the sculpture of Duane Hanson and John de Andrea, or it was replicated in materials foreign to its normal existence, a transformation that took it out of reality, as in the work of Marilyn Levine, Judd Nelson, and Fumio Yoshimura.[49] Castle's trompe l'oeil works display both of these types of illusionism. While the furniture was rendered in a superrealistic fashion, the objects were also carved in wood, thus making them transcend reality.

In general, most of Castle's contemporaries compared his work with that of the widely exhibited Japanese-born sculptor Fumio Yoshimura, who throughout the decade was carving superrealistic sculptures in wood of inanimate objects like typewriters, bicycles, and hot-dog carts. Castle, however, was quick to point out the difference in their work: Yoshimura worked in soft woods while Castle always used hardwoods. Since hardwoods are more difficult to carve, Castle felt that he had to display greater technical competence to create a truly illusionistic work. Essentially, Castle took illusionism one step beyond what was in vogue by having his illusionistic works retain their functional qualities. His tables, for instance, could still be used as tables.

Plate 19
Coatrack with Trench Coat, 1978, two views
(checklist no. 18)

55

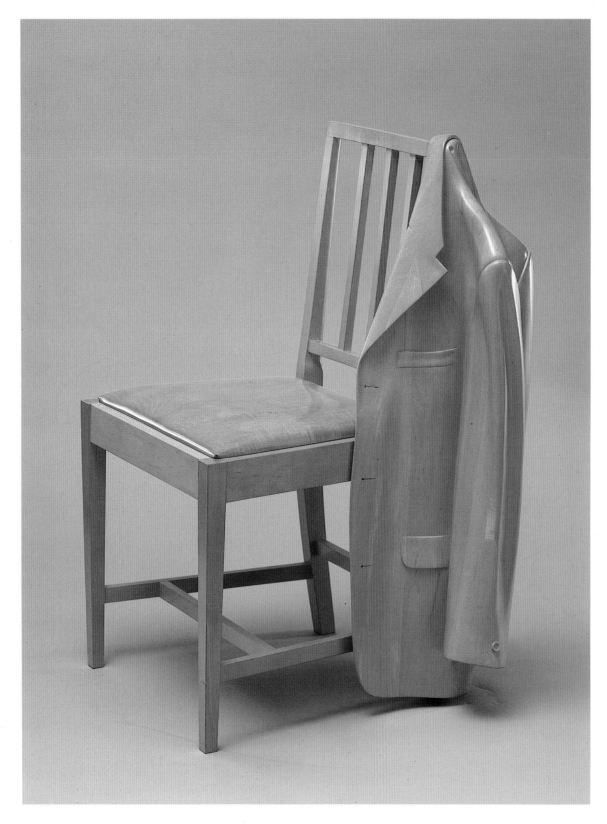

Plate 20
Chair with Sport Coat, 1978
(checklist no. 17)

Plate 21
Umbrella Stand, 1977
(checklist no. 16)

While Castle reworked several themes as part of the series, none of the trompe l'oeil sculptures was produced in a limited edition except for *Table with Gloves and Keys*, 1981 (pl. 40). Having carved one version in mahogany, Castle was commissioned to create a second one in a different wood, with a modified placement of the gloves and keys. Because he thought his patron wanted him to use an exotic wood, Castle chose purpleheart, a deep purplish wood also known as amaranth. This colorful table shocked the client since he, like most other people, was accustomed to red, brown, and blondish woods, and he refused to accept it, commissioning instead a third version, again in mahogany. (Ironically, purpleheart changes over time from a purple-red color to a brownish hue.)

Once again the craft world was the first to recognize the importance of this new sculptural direction. Castle's *Umbrella Stand* (pl. 21), the first of his trompe l'oeil pieces to be exhibited, was included in the prestigious show "Sixteen American Woodcarvers," organized in 1978 by studio craftsman Mark Lindquist for the Craft Center in Worcester, Massachusetts. Viewers were fascinated by the realism of Castle's illusionistic pieces. A review in a contemporary issue of *Craft Horizons* linked the work to the Pop Art movement of the 1960s.[50]

The first recognition that the illusionistic work received from the fine-arts world came that same year when Castle was invited to have a one-person show in a Soho space that the Cincinnati art dealer Carl Solway was sharing with Chicago dealer Phyllis Kind, Ruth Braunstein of San Francisco's Quay Gallery, and Edward Thorp, a California dealer. The director of Solway's space, Margarete Roeder, a friend of Castle since 1971, had suggested to the dealer that he exhibit Castle's new work since it tied in with the shows of the work of Peter Voulkos and Richard Shaw being organized for the space by Braunstein. Unfortunately, the response to the Castle show was poor; press coverage was minimal and there were no sales. Although illusionistic sculpture was still in vogue, Solway recalls that his clients at the time were more interested in following the emerging talents of the neo-expressionist painters Julian Schnabel and David Salle.

For the next two years the craft world continued to give this new sculptural work greater attention than did the fine-arts world. Both the Fendrick and Richard Kagan galleries prominently featured it in group shows.[51] In addition, two illusionistic works, *Umbrella Stand* and *Coatrack with Trench Coat*, were included in the American Craft Museum's 1979 exhibition "New Handmade Furniture."[52] Frustrated by the lack of recognition from the fine-arts world, Castle decided to look into various galleries in New York. Finally, in 1980, he approached Alexander F. Milliken, founder and owner of a Soho gallery, about showing his work.

His choice of Milliken would prove to be sound. The dealer aggressively promoted and advertised Castle's work, frequently taking out full-page advertisements in *Art in America* and *Artnews* to announce upcoming exhibitions. His experience as a fine-arts dealer with innumerable contacts in the art world was particularly beneficial, bringing patrons to the gallery from all over the country. Over the years, although Milliken may have questioned the salability of certain aspects of Castle's aesthetic, he continually provided him with a showcase for his most recent work.

Castle's relationship with Milliken began auspiciously. His first one-person exhibition at the gallery in 1981, of predominantly illusionistic work, was well received. The general

Detail of *Umbrella Stand*
(pl. 21)

public had difficulty understanding the work since people did not realize that such large sculpture could not be carved from one piece of wood. However, most of the works in the show had been sold when it closed after three and one-half weeks, and the exhibition generated considerable excitement in the fine-arts world. *Arts Magazine* reviewed the exhibition, discussing Castle's work in relation to that of 1970s illusionist sculptors such as ceramist Marilyn Levine. The article noted his ability to transform "known surfaces into ones that lie outside of our realm."[53] John Russell of the *New York Times* lauded Castle as both furniture maker and sculptor, comparing his work to that of the Surrealist René Magritte.[54]

CASTLE ESTABLISHES HIS SCHOOL

The late 1970s brought about other significant changes in Castle's career. The production line of chairs, settees, and tables and the new forays into fine furniture generated increased cash flow and there was a significant number of orders from private clients and museums, promising work for several years. To help organize the financial operation of his shop, Castle took on a business partner, Van Buren N. Hansford, Jr., and formed Wendell Castle, Inc., in 1980. In addition, the "New Handmade Furniture" exhibition at the American Craft Museum had prompted Castle once again to assess his place vis-à-vis other artists. The furniture produced by teachers and students at the established furniture programs at RIT, at the Rhode Island School of Design, and at Boston University under the Program in Artisanry was an enormous success at this show, and Castle followed the lead of these institutions: he set up his own school called the Wendell Castle Workshop (later the Wendell Castle School). Room for this venture had become available in 1979 when Castle and ceramic artist Nancy Jurs, whom he had married in 1971, moved from the soybean mill to a nearby country house, thereby freeing the space they had lived in, which was adjacent to Castle's own studio, machine room, and showroom, for use by students.

Castle's recognition of the important role of schools came at a time when he regretted his teaching duties at Brockport since they took him away from his burgeoning shop. Impressed by Makepeace's School for Craftsmen in Wood, which he had established at Parnham House in Beaminster, Dorset, England, in 1977, and encouraged by Stephen Proctor, Castle wished to provide an alternative to the existing American schools. The Wendell Castle Workshop opened in the fall of 1980. Rather than emphasize technique to the detriment of design or vice versa, Castle, Proctor, and Sottile developed a balanced program that combined aspects of both a traditional craft apprenticeship and the curriculum required for a fine-arts degree. Castle established a two-year curriculum much like that at Parnham House. Castle, like Makepeace, headed the school; by 1983 the dean and primary instructor was Proctor. The first year emphasized drawing and the mastery of hand tools, achieved through prescribed, self-contained projects that inculcated discipline and a step-by-step approach to design and execution. The second year consisted of more open-ended design exercises. Castle relied on Proctor and others in the workshop to do the bulk of the actual teaching, while he offered constructive criticism and led discussions on how to buy equipment and set up a shop, how to price work, and where to sell or market it. Visiting artists also gave talks to supplement the curriculum. This synergistic combination of academic exploration with training in the elements of business success was similar to the approach used by Makepeace.[55]

For the next eight years the school had an average annual enrollment of twenty-five. Having more skilled workers in the building had a significant influence on Castle's production. Students were occasionally hired during rush times, but more important was the tendency for several graduates each year to stay on for a while. Familiar with Castle's ideas, techniques, and expectations, these "postgraduates" provided essential assistance.[56]

By this time Castle felt comfortable with the changes he had made and was content with his growing reputation. A discussion of his illusionistic sculptures had been included in the 1980 book *Art in the Seventies*, by noted British art historian Edward Lucie-Smith.[57] That same year the Dayton Art Institute had selected *Chair with Sport Coat* (pl. 20) for the exhibition "Woodworks I: New American Sculpture." The show also included works by such well-known American sculptors as Louise Nevelson and H. C. Westermann. Castle was no doubt pleased that the catalogue essay compared his interest in cabinetry with that of Westermann.

THE FINE ART OF THE FURNITURE MAKER

In 1980 Castle's growing reputation in the New York art world and his new interest in work based on historical forms made him the appropriate candidate for a project initiated by Bret Waller, the new director of the Memorial Art Gallery in Rochester.[58] Inspired by the example of the National Gallery in London, Waller developed the concept for an exhibition of furniture for which a contemporary artist would serve as a curator. The purpose of this format was to give the museum viewer a non-art-historical insight into selected works of art. Waller first proposed the idea to Castle, who responded favorably, and then contacted a former colleague at the Metropolitan Museum of Art, Penelope Hunter-Stiebel. Together they agreed to organize an exhibition entitled "The Fine Art of the Furniture Maker" that would highlight the little-known European furniture usually kept in storage at the Metropolitan. In preparation for the show, Hunter-Stiebel and Castle examined a full range of European and Asian work from the sixteenth century through the 1920s. The resulting exhibition, which opened in Rochester in November 1981, consisted of works that Castle found "aesthetically satisfying, instructive, or otherwise interesting."[59] The catalogue that accompanied the exhibition included Castle and Hunter-Stiebel's discussion about each piece, a dialogue that provides rich insight into his interests and aesthetics at this point of his career.

The opportunity to examine and to think about historical furniture profoundly affected Castle. On a philosophical level, he was intrigued by the ideas behind French Art Nouveau and Art Deco furniture. While Art Nouveau furniture manifested an emphasis on design, Art Deco examples embodied a greater interest in precious materials and time-consuming craftsmanship. Castle particularly liked the streamlined forms and imagery of the Art Deco pieces as well as the designers' use of rich veneers to cover construction, their concern with finished appearance, even on the undersides and interiors, and the use of decorative metal mounts. For Castle, the fact that Art Deco furniture was then coming into vogue in New York indicated that this approach to furniture would be relevant in arriving at an aesthetic appropriate to the 1980s.

MORE IS MORE: HISTORICISM

Following the success of his trompe l'oeil work, Castle began to commit the time and energies of his entire shop to the creation of historically based furniture exquisitely made from expensive and exotic materials. Castle drew up the designs, coordinated the work, did some cabinetmaking himself, and made the final decisions, but he also relied on the individual talents of the other four or five craftsmen in the shop. In a letter to Milliken in February 1982, Castle's office manager, Ann Baker, indicated that the "superbly crafted" joinery of the new pieces would make them more salable and that the "new design slogan for the 1980s" in the Castle workshop was "MORE IS MORE."[60] To differentiate this work from that in his earlier styles, Castle called it "fine" furniture, since the craftsmanship involved resembles that commonly found in fine antique furniture.

Castle's first work in this new style was *Lady's Desk with Two Chairs*, 1981 (pl. 42), of English sycamore decorated with ebony and plastic dots. The artist intended that these pieces "pick up where Emile-Jacques Ruhlmann, the last of the great *ébénistes*, left off."[61] In particular, the French designer's extensive use of marquetry dots influenced Castle, who used eighty-five hundred dots in the suite. While the highly decorated surface treatment of this work closely identifies him with the so-called Pattern and Decoration movement in America,[62] Castle may also have been influenced by the work of Makepeace, who was at this time making similarly refined furniture based on historical forms. In his book *Furniture: A Concise History*, Edward Lucie-Smith praised a Makepeace Gothic chair made up of two thousand ebony pieces as "a deliberate *tour de force*, a demonstration of supreme mastery of technique."[63] Castle's suite sold for seventy-five thousand dollars, a price that far exceeded the usual price of American studio furniture.

Castle devoted the next two and one-half years to the fabrication of new furniture for a Milliken show that opened in March 1983. Two of the most stunning examples in the show, which included objects ranging in size from small jewelry boxes to large tables, were a *Demilune Table*, 1981 (pl. 22), and an *Octagonal-Based Table*, 1981 (pl. 23). The rosewood and ivory demilune table is part of a negative-positive pair—the other table being made of light sycamore with ebony decoration. The richly matched veneers, the use of ivory mounts and dots to emphasize ends and lines, the massive torus molding of the skirt, and the graceful curve of the legs all point to the influence of Ruhlmann. The entire underside was veneered and finished as well as the top. The clean, straightforward form, faceted edges, and light bird's-eye maple veneer of the *Octagonal-Based Table* recall the Biedermeier furniture of mid-nineteenth-century Germany, while its geometric patterning harks back to the work of the French *ébéniste*. To this essentially Germanic design, Castle added his own engineering wizardry. The faceted column tapers to a sharp point that rests on the base and relies upon ebony rings for support.

In looking at the Metropolitan Museum's collection for the 1981 exhibition, Castle had expressed keen interest in an Empire medal cabinet designed by Charles Percier. Castle was particularly taken by the cabinet's simple monolithic form, which he thought looked very contemporary. He also responded favorably to the French interpretation of Egyptian detailing of the cabinet. Castle's *Egyptian Humidor*, 1981 (pl. 24), reveals his own interpretation of the simple tapered mass and abstract Egyptian ornament of the Percier work. The combination of black and gold as a design element, seen in the humidor's inlaid frieze of

Plate 22
Demilune Table, 1981
(checklist no. 21)

Plate 23
Octagonal-Based Table, 1981
(checklist no. 24)

Plate 24
Egyptian Humidor, 1981
(checklist no. 22)

64

ebony and sycamore, was derived from a large desk designed by Louis Süe and André Mare around 1925, which Castle also became aware of as a result of his collaboration with Hunter-Stiebel. In combining aspects from these historical works, Castle created a humidor that raises cigar storage and preservation to a monumental level. The size, the architectural massing, and the rich materials of the humidor serve almost to obliterate its basic function. In fact, the humidor is supposedly a maquette, and an elaborate one at that, for an Empire-Egyptian desk that was never realized.

The brochure for the 1983 Milliken show became important as a marketing tool, emphasizing Castle's new philosophy of workmanship as art to the point of hyperbole. Captions list the exotic woods, such as Gabon ebony, describe the joinery, and enumerate the number of layers of hand-rubbed nitro-cellulose lacquer (the favored finish of Ruhlmann). At the time, Milliken stated that the beauty of Castle's work was the direct result of the depth of finesse, technique, and skill evident in the compulsive perfection of the joinery, the tight fit of the drawers, the finished undersides and backs, and the precision of the veneering.[64]

Some of Castle's work from 1983 and 1984 displays freer, more abstract references to the past. *Temple Desk and Chair*, 1984 (pl. 25), illustrates Castle's continued interpretation of the black-and-gold color scheme and metal mounts of Süe's and Mare's Art Deco desk as he transferred the color scheme to a design more inspired by Art Deco architecture and the irreverent, humorous style typical of the Italian design group MEMPHIS MILANO in the early 1980s. The sleek, geometrical shapes of the conical feet, the height of the legs, and the arched back of the chair bespeak a contemporary aesthetic. Castle combined lavish materials such as twenty-three-karat gold plating, ebonized imbuya veneer, Osage orange, and solid ebony, which he pushed to their technical limits to achieve the desired result.

Temple Desk and Chair is also important for its metal detailing. In December 1983 Castle invited Greg Bloomfield to join the Castle Workshop. Bloomfield brought with him an expertise in metalworking gained when he worked with the California furniture maker Garry Knox Bennett. Upon Bloomfield's arrival, Castle began to use more plated metal and brass in his designs.

Pleated Bookcase, 1984 (pl. 27), a commission resulting from the 1983 exhibition at Milliken's gallery, makes a visual pun on the 1920s and 1930s emphasis on herringbone veneer. By using two-dimensional herringbone veneer in the lower section and three-dimensional pleating in the upper section, Castle confuses the viewer and engages his/her attention. A more explicitly metaphorical intent is evident in *Pyramid Coffee Table*, 1984 (pl. 26). In this piece Castle interweaves the symbolism and connotations of three basic geometrical forms: the pyramid, the cone, and the obelisk. The sides of the pyramid open up to reveal a small obelisk, which can serve as a reference to Egyptian history or to the Washington Monument, or as a symbol of the ritual role of coffee drinking in America.

A more novel synthesis of historical and contemporary designs was Castle's *Late Proposal for the Rochester Convention Center in the Form of a Jewelry Box* of 1982 (fig. 15). While the figured-veneer carcass and brass mounts manifest the influence of Art Deco, the colored cone-and-donut legs reveal Castle's eye for contemporary shapes and colors. Many commentators consider this design to fall within the confines of Post-Modernism since the palette is very much like that of architects and designers working in

Figure 15
Wendell Castle, *Late Proposal for the Rochester Convention Center in the Form of a Jewelry Box*, 1982.

Plate 25
Temple Desk and Chair, 1984, two views
(checklist no. 29)

Plate 26
Pyramid Coffee Table, 1984, two views
(checklist no. 28)

Plate 27
Pleated Bookcase, 1984
(checklist no. 27)

this style, but it is more accurate to view the form as contemporary deco in that it recalls the soft-edged, streamlined masses and abstract details of the 1930s rather than the architectonic masses and classical details of Post-Modernism. Castle flatly states that he is not a Post-Modernist but a "historical classicist" who abhors the ironic qualities present in much Post-Modernist work.

FURTHER EFFORTS IN PRODUCTION FURNITURE

Like his mentors of the 1920s, Castle developed simple adaptations of his unique show pieces to be produced in limited editions. In 1982 he entered into an agreement with the Gunlocke Company of Wayland, New York, for four lines of office furniture that Castle would design, his workshop would build, and the furniture company would market. A year later he began to explore a similar relationship with Arc International, New York.[65]

Castle's agreement with Gunlocke called for a minimum of four furniture suites, each containing a selection of the following pieces: a desk, a credenza, a conference table, and side chairs. Each of the four lines was to have a different style: a Ruhlmann-type line with faceted torpedo legs called *Oneida* (fig. 16); a more Post-Modernist design with half-column legs and dentilled rails called *Olympus* (fig. 17); one with podlike legs called *Elysium* (fig. 18); and another with lacquered cone-and-donut legs like those on the Rochester Convention Center proposal. The last line, which was the first to be introduced, was called *Atlantis* and was available in lacewood (light), fiddleback maple (medium), and Tchitola (dark) veneers with the donut feet lacquered in either turquoise, peach, or magenta (pl. 28). The lacquer-finished legs are significant since they represent Castle's renewed interest in surface color. As in the Convention Center proposal, the colors are similar to those of Post-Modernist architecture, but the forms of the *Atlantis* line are less architectonic and more directly dependent on the function of the piece.

Figure 16
Wendell Castle, *Oneida Desk*, 1982/83, designed for
the Gunlocke Company.

Figure 17
Wendell Castle, *Olympus Desk*, 1982/83, designed
for the Gunlocke Company.

Figure 18
Wendell Castle, *Elysium Desk*, 1982/83, designed for
the Gunlocke Company.

Plate 28
Prototype for Atlantis Desk, 1982
(checklist no. 26)

CLOCKS

About 1983 Milliken urged Castle to develop a project in which the works would not be solely defined by their function as furniture. In response to this advice, Castle undertook a group of unique tall clocks, ranging in height from six to eight feet, in which his intention was to explore the theme of time. He hoped that this conceptual approach would provide a counterweight to the emphasis on technical excellence that he feared might lead to his being labeled just a "furniture maker."

This decision was based in part on his interest in representational sculpture and in part on the personnel in his shop. Since 1969, when he had written an article for *Craft Horizons* on the work of the American sculptor Mike Nevelson, Castle had been fascinated with the form and significance of the grandfather clock. Castle felt that the strength of Nevelson's work lay in the fact that he saw a clock not just as a timepiece but as a monumental sculpture with strong anthropomorphic qualities. Nevelson's work had additional relevance for Castle as it frequently addressed the issue of form following function.[66] Both Milliken and Castle probably felt that by developing a series of monumental clocks with sculptural qualities, they could continue marketing Castle's work as sculpture. Clocks were the logical synthesis and extension of the earlier trompe l'oeil works and his more recent fine furniture.

The makeup of his workshop also played a role in Castle's new direction because he knew he had the necessary special skills at his command. Peter Pierobon, a former student who joined the shop in 1983, Sottile, and others had the cabinetmaking skills for the carcasses; Bloomfield provided the expertise for metal fabrication such as plating and casting; and William Sloane, an engineer by training who arrived in March 1983, was extremely talented in designing and milling hardware and mechanisms. Castle's confidence in this group gave him the freedom to pursue the clock theme on various levels, both functional and metaphorical.

Castle's intention of producing a series of conceptual pieces was ambitious. His original idea was to investigate the various levels of meaning inherent in the concept of time, but he ended up exploring the several ways in which the form of a clock can be viewed: architecturally, anthropomorphically, and metaphorically. Ten of his clocks are concerned with the architectonic and monumental qualities of timepieces. Whether he drew his design ideas from Sumerian temples (*Ziggurat*; fig. 19), the Egyptian sun deity Horus (*Sun God*, fig. 20), or the geometric forms of the French architect Claude-Nicolas Ledoux (*Mystery*), Castle's approach to these clocks was architectural in terms of their mass and historical in terms of their detailing. Castle's ultimate concern for function is manifested in the attention devoted to the clocks' dials and hands. However, while most have well-articulated mechanisms, a few of the clocks strongly question function. For example, *Sun God* has no dial and the hands are so small in relation to the entire composition that their presence appears to be an afterthought, while *Ghost* (pl. 30) is totally nonfunctional.

The ten architectonic clocks are closely related to Castle's fine furniture. The influence of his study of Art Deco furniture is evident in his reliance on exotic and figured veneers to provide lines and coloring in the composition of the mass. Similarly, the cones, columns, and triangular forms that made up the vocabulary of his Post-Modernist furniture of 1983–84 reappear in many of these clocks. One significant change, however, was in their construction. For his earlier fine furniture, Castle used Baltic birch plywood to provide a flat,

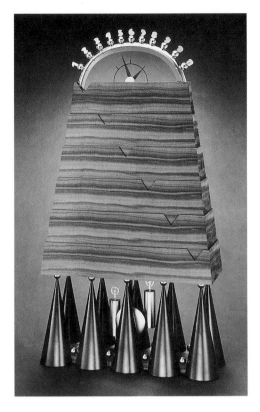  

stable base for the veneered surfaces. Beginning in 1982 he began to use Canadian-made flakeboard. The change in materials reflects Castle's increased interest in surface appearance and decoration. Castle's craftsmen joined the mitered-and-butted joints of these laminates and composites by cutting circular slots with a router and then placing compressed wooden "biscuits" or plates in these slots. When glue was applied and the pieces clamped together, the biscuits swelled and formed a strong spline joint. This joinery technique, which began to be used in studio furniture making only around 1982, was ideal for large, awkward joints and for complex angles. Its simplicity and high degree of accuracy also made this technique ideal for craftsmen who wished to save time and avoid complicated or fussy joinery. Plate joinery thus allowed Castle to spend more time on finish and the engineered parts.[67]

While the ten architectonic clocks drew from earlier ideas and motifs, the other three clocks embodied a new direction. *Four Years before Lunch* (fig. 21) and *Jester* (pl. 29) are explorations of the anthropomorphic qualities of clocks. *Jester* was the first full manifestation of the human figure to appear in Castle's work since the abstract figurative sculptures of the early 1960s. It was a figure, however, executed with sophisticated cabinetmaking techniques, evident most clearly in the execution of the jester's garment. The alternating patterns of imbuya and fiddleback mahogany veneers are enhanced by the grain patterns of the wood in the individual diamond shapes.

Jester is significant not only because it represents the beginning of a body of work exploring the human figure but also because it stresses strong narrative imagery over function and over material. As in his earlier glass-reinforced lamps, Castle emphasized the

Figure 19
Wendell Castle, *Ziggurat*, 1985.

Figure 20
Wendell Castle, *Sun God*, 1985.

Figure 21
Wendell Castle, *Four Years before Lunch*, 1984.

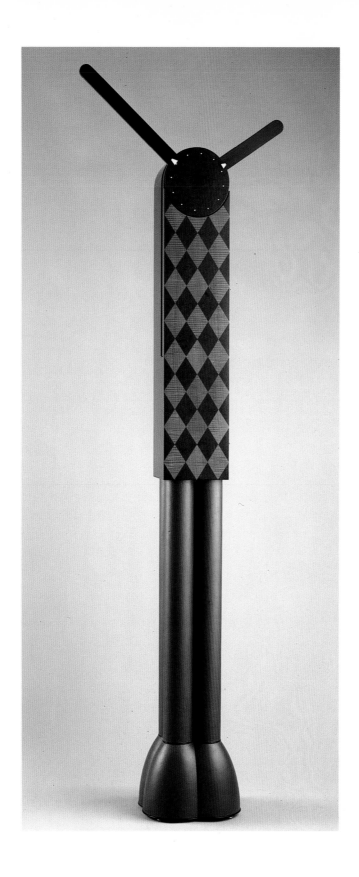

Plate 29
Jester, 1985
(checklist no. 31)

76

sculptural significance of the clocks by giving them specific titles. He de-emphasized the sensual qualities of the wood by either painting the surfaces or encasing them in leather. In *Jester* Castle chose to emphasize the human qualities of the form by covering the wooden legs with leather.

Ghost (pl. 30) is the most radical statement among Castle's thirteen original clocks because it is completely nonfunctional. Directly inspired by an eighteenth-century tall case clock that Castle had borrowed from an antique-dealer friend, *Ghost* is reminiscent of Castle's trompe l'oeil work. As he had in the *Chair with Sport Coat* (pl. 20), in *Ghost* Castle combined an actual piece of furniture with the illusion of a fabric executed in wood. However, while it is apparent that the sport coat is made of wood, thus rendering the illusion of fabric incomplete, the sheet that supposedly drapes the clock is made of mahogany that has been bleached in order to make the counterfeit more complete. The primary significance of *Ghost* lies in the fact that, although it displays an affinity with the work of such contemporary illusionists as Levine, Hanson, and de Andrea, it is nevertheless successful as a representation of a piece of furniture. *Ghost* is yet another example of Castle's inclination for using the functional as a point of departure for exploring the nonfunctional.

The clocks, some of which were included in two traveling exhibitions, drew enormous public response.[68] National and international newspapers and magazines ran articles about them and their maker. The writings focused on the clocks' scale and imagery and on Castle's successful union of the fine arts, craft, and architecture. The works were being discussed not in terms of whether they were art or craft but rather whether they were sculpture or furniture. Along with the artistic significance of the clocks, the articles also highlighted the high prices of the clocks, ranging from seventy-five thousand dollars to two-hundred-fifty thousand dollars. Such prices seemed to add to the excitement surrounding Castle's work at the time. After the opening of the Whitney Museum of American Art's exhibition "High Styles: Twentieth-Century American Design," in which two of Castle's works were included, a Florida newspaper dubbed 1985 the "Year of Wendell Castle."[69]

In spite of their overall popularity, the clocks engendered some of the strongest negative criticism that Castle had ever received. In the magazine *Fine Woodworking*, Roger Holmes discussed the failure of most of the clocks as sculpture. Admitting that the pieces were clever as curios or objets d'art, he found them "banal, clichéd, or incoherent" as sculpture.[70] To Holmes, the clocks were a mishmash of thinly derived, heavy-handed, and competing images. Anthony Urbane Chastain-Chapman, writing in the magazine *American Craft*, found the clocks to be lacking in design and workmanship as well. In his opinion, there was little coherence in the forms and detailing, and the works, their cases, and their veneers manifested a variety of levels of technical achievement.[71] Both Holmes and Chastain-Chapman felt that the clocks' importance lay not in the success of their individual designs or in their technical competence but rather in Castle's overall vision. Other furniture makers might surpass Castle in either technique or composition, but none could match Castle's ability to commit himself to such a large project that would have such a dramatic impact upon the public and the field.

During the run of the 1985–86 traveling show "Masterpieces of Time," organized by the Taft Museum in Cincinnati, Castle discontinued the series of clocks. Dismayed that the

Plate 30
Ghost, 1985
(checklist no. 30)

thirteen original clocks had not engendered any positive critical reviews from the art world, he was also frustrated that the project was not economically profitable.

WORK OF THE MID-1980S

Before Castle began his series of fine furniture in 1981, his work could not be compared with that of sculptors like Scott Burton, Lucas Samaras, Vito Acconci, and Richard Artschwager, who were creating sculptural furniture that was essentially metaphorical rather than utilitarian. While these artists stressed the conceptual, Castle had continued to stress the virtues of his medium and thereby remained a woodworker in most critics' eyes, even though his forms were unconventional. Although his Ruhlmann-inspired fine furniture represented a definite break with his craft background, since by reinterpreting these historical designs he gave them a metaphorical twist, and the clock series had definite symbolic overtones, in both groups the functional aspect remained uppermost. Thus, in the mid-1980s Castle decided to adapt his aesthetic to resemble even more closely the goal of these sculptors: to create works that stress intellectual content over function and medium. He suppressed his earlier concerns with organic form, materials, and historical design and began to concentrate on expression.

For his own dining table (pl. 31) of 1985, Castle designed a table surface that consists of a rich holly veneer, inlaid purpleheart triangles, and dots that form the words of Henry Ford II's famous aphorism, "Never complain, never explain." The surface is supported on leather-wrapped wooden cones, and below the skirt run two decorative purpleheart forms with gold-plated rings at either end. The combination of fine veneering, lively, colorful decoration, and nonwood coverings on the supports is Castle at his best in the mid-1980s. The table is also significant because it marks the return of his use of words as imagery.

Increasing his efforts to create forms that are symbolic rather than utilitarian, Castle began to paint and stain his surfaces. In the early 1960s Castle had executed several large Abstract Expressionist paintings, one of which he had retained in his private collection. In 1968–69 he had painted the Fiberglas surfaces of his stack-laminated furniture with automotive enamel. Finally, in 1984, pleased with the painted interior of the *Dr. Caligari* clock (fig. 22), and with the encouragement of Sottile, Castle decided to make decorated surfaces an important compositional element in his work. His interest in elaborate surface treatment shows his continuing involvement with the Pattern and Decoration movement as well as his response to the work of other studio furniture makers, such as Alphonse Mattia and Tom Loeser, who were also using color and pattern.

The *Dr. Caligari Desk and Chair* of 1986 (pl. 32) is one of Castle's most successful experiments in integrating form and surface decoration. Reminiscent of a desk created in 1931 by Esherick, the desk and chair were designed with sharp, angular forms and abrupt corners.[72] Castle decided to heighten the Cubist feeling of the form by applying black and white paint to it using the kind of brushstroke typical of the Abstract Expressionist painter Franz Kline. In order to emphasize the importance of the painted surface, Castle reused the title of his first painted clock, *Dr. Caligari*, which in turn refers to the film *The Cabinet of Dr. Caligari*, whose angular set designs had been the source of his inspiration. Because Sottile was eager to paint furniture, the artist decided to allow him to work on this particular

Figure 22
Wendell Castle, *Dr. Caligari*, 1984. Rochester, New York, University of Rochester, Memorial Art Gallery, Given in honor of Joan M. Vanden Brul by her family (88.1).

79

Plate 31
Never Complain, Never Explain, 1985, two views
(checklist no. 32)

grouping. Sottile's application of the water-soluble stain with a brush drawn roughly over the surface produced a watercolor effect.

Although several innovative exhibitions had been organized in the 1970s on the emergence of furniture as an art form,[73] the publication in 1984 of Denise Domergue's book *Artists Design Furniture* focused the general public's attention on the significance of the functional and nonfunctional furniture that artists, architects, and craftsmen were creating.[74] It was in this atmosphere, in 1986, that Castle once again began a series of basically nonfunctional tables and cabinets.

The Music of Rubber Bands, 1986 (pl. 33), one of the earliest of the "warped-top table" series, had its origins in hall-table design. Castle recently noted: "A hall table is not really used. It sits there in the hall and is supposed to look beautiful. You may put your gloves on it, or a piece of mail, but you don't really use it. These pieces are meant to act like hall tables, take up that same space, but do it in a much more expressive way than conventional tables do."[75] The inspiration for these warped tops was the fabrication of warped-top benches by Castle's assistant Graham Campbell. The success of these benches resulted in a warped-top theme for the 1986 faculty show of the Wendell Castle School at the Dawson Gallery in Rochester, New York. *The Music of Rubber Bands* denies many of the elements that normally constitute table design. The upwardly curved tabletop rests on two pointed legs. Most of the support for the entire structure is provided by the downwardly curved organic stretcher bars that break with traditional design and reach the floor. Castle emphasizes the form over the beauty of the woods through the jarring juxtaposition of the lighter lacewood veneer of the bent-laminated top with the ebonized cherry of the scarf-laminated structure. In later warped tables Castle achieved the same end by painting the wood and adding aluminum, rubber, or wooden vessels.

The cabinets of this period also call into question traditional ideas about the structure of a piece of furniture. They are usually small, not particularly functional cabinets that are supported by an artistic imitation of an actual object, like a ladder, a set of steps, or a plant, which has no apparent thematic relation to the cabinet.[76] Works like *Untitled (Potted Rubber Tree)*, 1986 (pl. 34), with its absurd juxtaposition of a potted rubber plant and a yellow, barely functional cabinet, were not meant for storage but as objects of contemplation. In both the warped-top tables and the cabinets, Castle relied on lamination techniques and plate joinery, rejecting the fastidious cabinetmaking techniques he had acquired in the 1970s. This approach was an important element of his quest to transcend the confines of fine furniture. The critics immediately understood this; they saw this body of work as sculpture.[77]

Castle's *Humidor* of 1987 (pl. 35) is important because it attests to the success of this approach to the cabinet form. Having developed a basic formula for the structure of a cabinet, the artist adapted it to other uses. The *Humidor* is supported on a set of steps, but the normally rectilinear container has been replaced by three ovular forms sandwiched between two rectangular blocks of wood. The *Humidor*'s scale, its exterior form, and its boldly painted surface of layered enamels completely obscure its function, providing no indication that the upper blue form opens to reveal the traditional Lebanese cedar interior of a humidor.

Plate 32
Dr. Caligari Desk and Chair, 1986
(checklist no. 33)

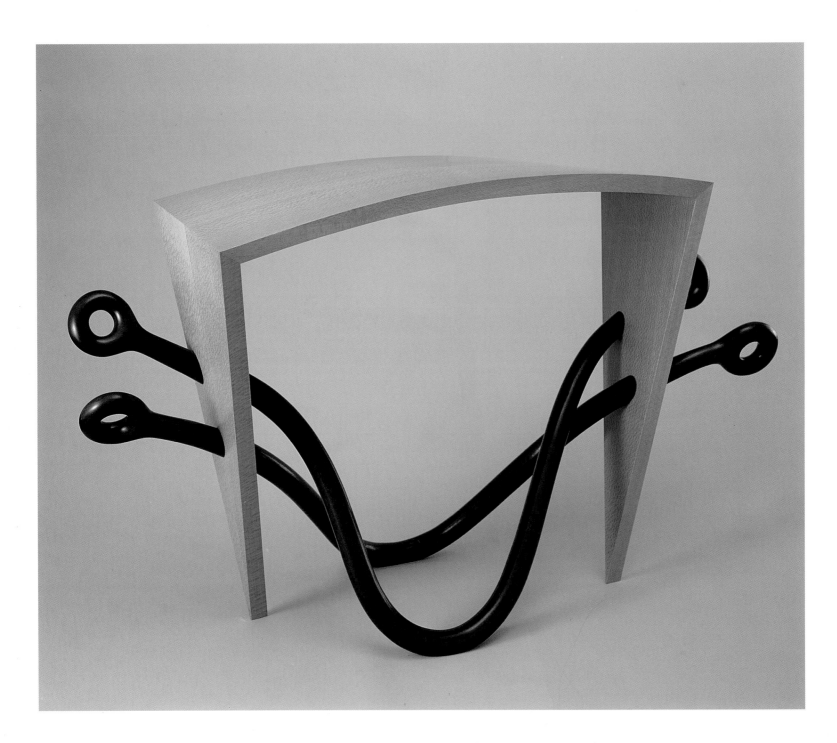

Plate 33
The Music of Rubber Bands, 1986
(checklist no. 34)

84

Plate 34
Untitled (Potted Rubber Tree), 1986
(checklist no. 35)

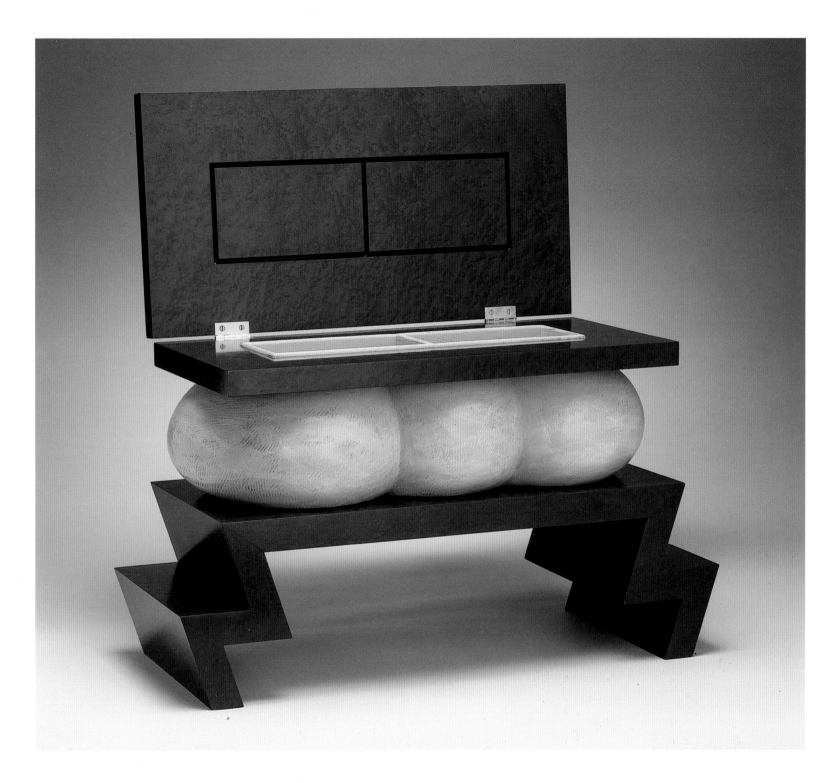

Plate 35
Humidor, 1987, two views
(checklist no. 36)

Plate 36
Library, 1987–88,
for the residence of Peter T. Joseph, New York

88

The introduction of these semifunctional painted forms brought a positive response from the museum world. Since 1976 Castle's stack-laminated and early fine furniture forms have been gradually accessioned into museum collections, including those of the Metropolitan Museum of Art; the Museum of Fine Arts, Boston; the Brooklyn Museum; the Philadelphia Museum of Art; the Museum of Fine Arts, Houston; and the Memorial Art Gallery of the University of Rochester. Much of his fine furniture and many of his clocks were acquired by corporations or individual collectors. Within a short time after the warped-top tables and the cabinets were first exhibited, some of the same institutions that had made a previous commitment to Castle's work purchased an example of this new work.[78] Other museums, including the Milwaukee Art Museum and the Hunter Museum of Art in Chattanooga, Tennessee, began their collections of Castle's work with objects from these series.

Castle received the most support for this work from a new breed of decorative-arts collectors, people whose sustained purchasing differentiated them from the occasional buyers of the 1960s and 1970s: among these were prominent collectors like Sydney and Frances Lewis, Ronald and Anne Abramson, and Peter T. Joseph. However, these collectors primarily purchased existing works from galleries; in general, Castle received very few commissions from private individuals during this period.

Castle's most important commission from the private sector came from Joseph. In 1987, having seen the built-in bookcases and shelves that Castle had designed in 1984 for Alexander Milliken's apartment, Joseph asked Castle to design a library in his New York apartment.[79] Castle's completed room (pl. 36) strongly challenges accepted notions of design by blurring distinctions between the parts of the architectural skin and upsetting the functional arrangement of the storage spaces. Gesso is the unifying element; the entire upper portion of the walls is covered with panels of gesso decorated with swirling, circular patterns in low relief. These panels serve both as wall covering and as doors; it is impossible to differentiate one from the other. When the cabinets are open, bookcases and cabinets are revealed, which form acute and obtuse angles with the ceiling and the floor in a fashion that causes one at first glance to question their ability to hold objects. The covered cabinets and slanted bookshelves sit astride a shelf that runs in disjointed, angular fashion up, down, and around the perimeter of the room. Below the shelf is a beautifully pieced together wall covering, again doubling as disguised doors, made of asymmetric, angular pieces of satin-wood buffed to a soft sheen. The overall effect conveys a feeling of warmth and richness in an environment that is somewhat destabilizing and anarchic. The room is reminiscent of the den of Dr. Caligari, and in that regard is the most fully developed of Castle's Caligari works (see fig. 22 and pl. 32). Castle's use of these skewed cabinets links the entire environment to Deconstructivist architecture of the 1980s, with its basic tenet that architecture should recognize and acknowledge the impurities inherent in all structures rather than impose an unnatural order and harmony on them.

PUBLIC COMMISSIONS

Given the limitations of private commissions, Castle has turned his attention to large-scale public art. His ability over the past few years to attract commissions for works in highly visible settings is a testament to both the quality of his work and the acceptance of the art-furniture movement in America. Since 1986 Castle has received commissions for three clocks for public spaces, a commemorative piano, and seating for two public art museums.[80] These projects have forced Castle to develop a new aesthetic, one that combines strong, monumental, sometimes minimalistic forms with function. His approach to public commissions is similar to that of the new generation of public sculptors. Like Scott Burton, Siah Armajani, Mary Miss, Nancy Holt, Andrew Leicester, and Joyce Kozloff, Castle creates sculptures that are integrated into their settings rather than being a challenge to them. Castle and these other artists design works that are intended to be inviting, works to which the public can relate and with which it can interact in some way. Since public response and ease of maintenance are important factors in public works, Castle cannot experiment as freely as in his earlier work. He has simplified his "more is more" vocabulary to make his work friendlier and used his craftsman's knowledge of materials to provide the strong contrasts necessary if the works are to stand out in large spaces.

The clock commissioned in 1987 for the foyer of the Maccabees Life Insurance Company in Southfield, Michigan, was the first of Castle's public art commissions to integrate form successfully with environment (pl. 37). Castle had wanted the company to commission *Portraits of Grandmother and Grandfather*, his initial proposal for two modified *Jester* clocks with brightly patterned garments to be placed on either side of the foyer of the Maccabees building. Instead, the company selected a proposal for a more conservative piece that directly responded to the architecture. Castle's realized design consists of a gold-leaf clock mounted on four elongated cone forms, which in turn are attached to a circular base. Castle covered the tall cones with leather to minimize the sensuousness of the wood. His decision to emphasize the horizontal and vertical patterning of the gold-leaf face of the clock and the verticality of the cones is particularly relevant for this commission since both elements reiterate the foyer's skin of square maple panels outlined in American walnut and punctuated by narrow columns of maple striated with walnut.

The *500,000th Commemorative Steinway Piano and Bench* (pl. 38) commissioned in 1987 by Steinway & Sons is another conservative work. Since the piano was required to have the excellent audio qualities for which Steinway pianos are known, Castle could make few alterations in its actual form. He was able to modify the basic shape of the legs and the rim and to adjust the position of all three legs. However, Castle's major contribution to the design of the piano is in its surface decoration. Asked to incorporate the signatures of the 832 concert pianists currently performing on Steinways, Castle inlaid the signatures into strips of East Indian ebony and dyed Swiss pear veneers, which were then wrapped around the exterior of the piano. To the extent that they are decorative elements tying the entire composition together, the archival significance of the signatures is negated. When the piano is placed in a large concert hall, viewers see only the striped effect of the beautiful veneers.

Plate 37
Untitled, 1988
(checklist no. 41)

Detail of
500,000th Commemorative Steinway Piano and Bench
(pl. 38)

The *Bench* (pl. 43) commissioned in 1986 by the Detroit Institute of Arts provided Castle with several important challenges. Castle wanted to create a functional seating unit that embodied many of the concerns of his work over the past thirty years yet one that could withstand considerable use. At first, he envisioned this as an opportunity to further his experiments with bronze and aluminum surfaces. The artist had become interested in aluminum after accepting an invitation to participate in an exhibition of furniture made from aluminum organized by the Kaiser Center Art Gallery in Oakland, California, in 1986, and he already knew of Garry Knox Bennett's and Jerry Carniglia's success with aluminum furniture. The addition of metalworker William Schaefer to his workshop in the summer of 1987 enabled Castle seriously to consider further work in this medium. Initially, Castle proposed a bench consisting of two upholstered seating elements supported by an aluminum frame and with either bronze or painted wooden legs.

Then, realizing that the bench would be the first major work of his to enter Detroit's collection, Castle rethought his design so that it would incorporate some of the significant concerns of his career. He wanted to design a bench that would make a strong statement but would not overpower the other works of art in the gallery where it would be exhibited. Castle's solution is a bench consisting of two attached seating elements that resemble the

Plate 38
500,000th Commemorative Steinway Piano and Bench, 1988
(checklist no. 39)

boat-shaped beds of the Empire period. A brushed-aluminum framework is supported by legs and armrests carved of purpleheart; this combination gives the bench a strong coloristic presence and displays the artist's continuing interest in exotic woods. For the organically shaped armrests Castle returned to stack lamination and a technique that resembled bricklaying, which he had used in some of his earlier works.

Of all the commissions that Castle has recently received, the one in 1987 from Hammerson Canada, Inc., a real-estate development company in Toronto, for a piece of outdoor sculpture is the most successful in inviting public interaction with the work of art. It also represents a paradigm for Castle's future work in the area of functional public art. Castle's proposal uses the idea of a tall case clock as a starting point. Certain elements of the design are directly related to the origins of the piece in this traditional clock form: its dual rounded dials and accentuated hands and the relationship between its rather small face and long narrow vertical body (see pl. 39). But here the similarities end. The design challenges accepted notions of what a timepiece should look like. The sculpture's lack of decoration, the geometry of its parts, and its monumentality (it is nineteen feet high) are reminiscent of Minimalist sculpture of the 1960s and 1970s. Yet, in contrast with the work of Donald Judd and other Minimalist sculptors, the sculpture has a warm, friendly demeanor, primarily due to the rich coloristic effect caused by the juxtaposition of patinated bronze, brushed stainless steel, and gold-leafed aluminum. Castle hopes that its placement on the sidewalk and the height of the various elements will encourage people to walk under the legs (see frontispiece). He notes, "People can literally meet you under the clock."[81]

In 1989 Castle is at a propitious moment in his career. The tall, soft-spoken, graying yet energetic man realizes his importance as a leader in the Studio Craft movement and in the fight for acceptance of craft into the mainstream of American art. That the Studio Craft movement is now being viewed as a legitimate movement existing alongside Abstract Expressionism, Minimalism, and other postwar developments represents a recognition that the traditional division of creative work into strictly defined categories of fine art, decorative art, and craft is no longer valid. Castle, like many other studio craftsmen today, firmly believes that his work should be placed within the larger context of twentieth-century art. Like Constantin Brancusi, Henry Moore, Wharton Esherick, and Charles and Ray Eames before him, he uses wood to create new, highly expressive forms.

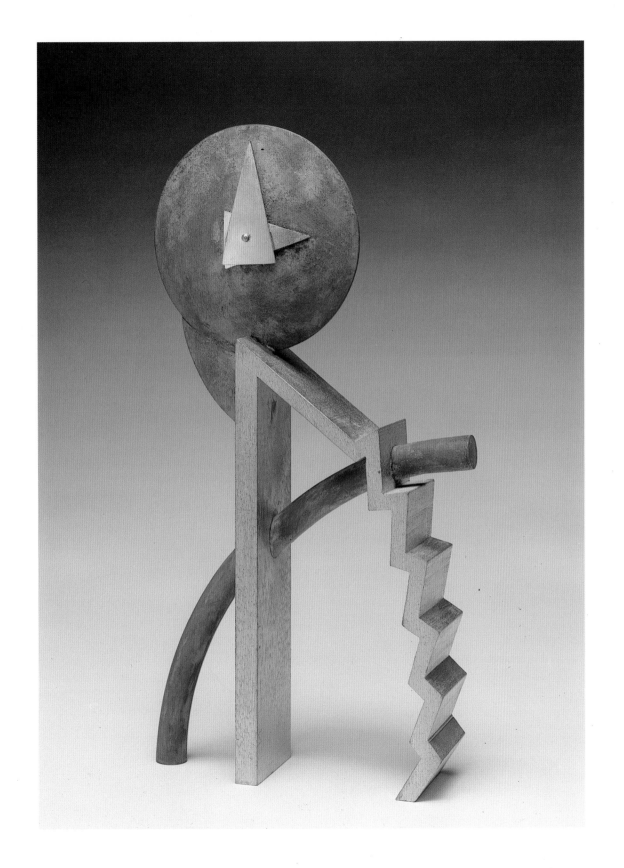

Plate 39
Maquette for Full Moon, 1987–88
(checklist no. 37)

95

1. For general biographical information on Wendell Castle, see *University Daily Kansan* 1961, *Who's Who* 1982–83, Chapman 1983, Stone 1986, and Netsky 1986a. A detailed account of Castle's course work at Baker University and the University of Kansas is provided in a letter from Don Scheid, Associate Dean, School of Fine Arts, University of Kansas, to Davira S. Taragin, October 20, 1988 (Detroit Institute of Arts Archives).

2. Don Wallance, *Shaping America's Products* (New York: Reinhold, 1956).

3. Castle 1970, 11.

4. Quoted in Washington 1972, 22.

5. For works by Nelson, Ponti, and Hoj, see Klaus-Jurgen Sembach, *Contemporary Furniture* (London: Design Council, 1982), 24, 29–31, 34–36; for the Donovan chair, see *Craft Horizons* 19 (March/April 1959): 21.

6. For Le Corbusier's chaise longue, see Sembach 1982 (note 5, above), 17. Kagan's rocker is illustrated in a review of a Kagan retrospective exhibition in the *New York Times* (April 17, 1980), 61.

7. See especially the stair in Esherick's house (1930), the sculpture *Defense* (1939), and a dressing-table stool (1947) reproduced in *The Wharton Esherick Museum: Studio and Collection* (Paoli, Pa.: Wharton Esherick Museum, 1984), cover, 24, 29.

8. For music stands by Castle, Esherick, Sam Maloof, and Art Carpenter, see Washington 1972, 14, 26, 34, 42. For additional illustrations of this popular form, see Dona Z. Meilach, *Woodworking: The New Wave* (New York: Crown Publishers, 1981), 112; *Fine Woodworking: Biennial Design Book* (Newtown, Conn.: Taunton Press, 1981); and *Fine Woodworking: Design Book Two* (Newtown, Conn.: Taunton Press, 1979).

9. Quoted in Stone 1986, 118.

10. See Frazier 1960.

11. *Scribe's Stool* is illustrated and discussed in several reviews of the exhibition. See Caplan 1962, Chapman 1962, Untracht 1962, *Home Furnishings Daily* 1962, and *House and Garden* 122 (October 1962): 164–165.

12. Metalsmith John Prip, cabinetmaker Frid, Pearson, and Wildenhain established Shop One in Rochester, New York, in 1952 as an outlet for their own production. Soon other local craftsmen, including Hans Christensen and Robert Donovan, were invited to become associate members. The shop remained one of the major sales outlets in the country until it closed in 1977. Castle had one-person shows there in 1969 and 1974, and his work was also included in the show "Five Owners," which focused on the work of the artists who owned the gallery in 1972: Castle, Wildenhain, Pearson, Thomas Markusen, and Barbara Cowles. For a short time in 1976, Shop One utilized some of the space in the Scottsville soybean mill in which Castle lived and worked.

13. Quoted in Seattle 1968, 49.

14. The best discussions of Castle's lamination techniques are found in his own book (Castle and Edman 1980), Kelsey 1976, and Castle 1976.

15. Quoted in Seattle 1968, 49.

16. Quoted in Washington 1972, 38.

17. Included in Castle's papers at the Archives of American Art is an underscored article on Sugarman by Amy Goldin that appeared in the June 1966 issue of *Arts Magazine*. Castle's article "Wood: George Sugarman" appeared in *Craft Horizons* 27 (March 1967): 30–33.

18. The exhibition consisted of eleven recent works and thirty drawings. A number of the works in the show, including *Library Sculpture* and *Desk and Chair* (both 1965), were sold; in fact, sales exceeded six thousand dollars. Half of the exhibition was subsequently shown in 1966 at the Renaissance Society of the University of Chicago, along with the work of Esherick, Maloof, and Marcelo Grassman. Several other works were incorporated into the "Fantasy Furniture" exhibition held at the Museum of Contemporary Crafts in New York, January 21–March 13, 1966. In the latter show, Castle's works were juxtaposed with those of Thomas Simpson, Pedro Friedeberg, Fabio de Sanctis, and Ugo Sterpini. See McKinley 1966.

19. Quoted in Giambruni 1968a, 31.

20. Other American craftsmen represented in the exhibition were Toshiko Takaezu (ceramics), Irena Brynner (jewelry), and Glen Michaels (mosaic). See Stina Kobell, "Stuttgart: International Crafts Exhibition," *Craft Horizons* 26 (September/October 1966): 23–27.

21. For reviews of the "Fantasy Furniture" exhibition, see *Craft Horizons* 1966, *Interior Design* 1966, Kelly 1966, O'Brien 1966, Page 1966, and *Progressive Architecture* 1966.

22. Letter from Nordness to *Cue* magazine, March 22, 1968, Nordness Papers, Archives of American Art.

NOTES

For a discussion of the development of furniture within the Studio Craft movement, see Boston, Museum of Fine Arts, *New American Furniture: Second Generation Studio Furnituremakers* (text by Edward S. Cooke, Jr.), 1989. Much valuable material on Castle's career can be found in the Wendell Castle Papers and the Lee Nordness Papers, Archives of American Art, Smithsonian Institution, Washington, D.C. Permission to quote from items in the Archives' collection of his personal papers has been graciously granted by Lee Nordness. Wendell Castle kindly made his archives in Scottsville, New York, available to the authors, as did gallery owners Alexander F. Milliken and Barbara Fendrick.

In addition, the following individuals provided important insights and information in interviews during research for this book: Wendell Castle, Graham Campbell, Barbara Fendrick, Penelope Hunter-Stiebel, Nancy Jurs, Richard Kagan, Martin Z. Margulies, Alexander F. Milliken, Lee Nordness, Albert Paley, Lorry Parks, Stephen Proctor, Ruth Raible, Victor von Reventlow, Margarete Roeder, Paul J. Smith, Carl Solway, Donald Sottile, Betty Tinlot, Bret Waller, and Ross Young.

In these notes, shortened citations consisting of either the author's name or the periodical/newspaper title plus the date of publication (for books and articles) or city and date (for exhibition catalogues) have been used for items that appear in full form in the Exhibition History and Bibliography sections at the back of this book.

23. See *Newsweek* 1968, Reif 1968a, and Simon 1968.

24. In April 1968 Nordness sent letters to the following artist-craftsmen, inviting them to exhibit in his gallery: Anni Albers, Clayton Bailey, F. Carlton Ball, Kenneth Bates, Fred Bauer, Hans Christensen, Wharton Esherick, Henry Halem, Judi Halem, Brent Kington, Freda Koblick, Bruno LaVerdière, Harvey Littleton, Sam Maloof, Joel Myers, John Paul Miller, Otto and Gertrud Natzler, Ronald Pearson, John Prip, Merry Renk, Ed Rossbach, Alice Shannon, Paul Soldner, Lenore Tawney, William Underhill, Peter Voulkos, Marguerite Wildenhain, and William Wyman. By 1971 he boasted of a stable of fifteen craftsmen representing all media. See "New York Galleries: Lee Nordness," *Arts Magazine* 45 (April 1971): 71; and letter from Nordness to Castle, April 10, 1968, Nordness Papers, Archives of American Art.

25. See *Art in America* 56 (September/October 1968): 7.

26. The Sachs display, entitled "An International Adventure in Advanced Seating Concepts," took place in March 1968 at their store on Thirty-fifth Street and Eighth Avenue in New York. Upon the recommendation of Paul J. Smith, Castle's *Double Chair* (1967, Collection of Wendell Castle) was one of the twenty chairs exhibited. In 1969 Nordness placed on consignment with Abraham & Straus two pieces of furniture by Castle as well as works by Jacqueline Ward, Harvey Littleton, David Kuraoka, Bill Stewart, Bob Stocksdale, Glen Kaufman, Patrick McCormick, and Regnor Reinholtsen.

27. The exhibition, entitled "The Furniture of Wendell Castle," opened in May 1969 at the Wichita Art Museum and then traveled to the University of Kansas Museum of Art, Lawrence (July 11–August 24, 1969), and the Louisville Art Center Association (September 3–23, 1969). Although it had been offered to museums all around the country, Richard Teitz, director of the Wichita Art Museum, was able to secure only these three venues, which is indicative of the lack of interest in contemporary craft at that time.

28. For details of Hanes's patronage of Castle, see letter from Nordness to Castle, January 13, 1968, Nordness Papers, Archives of American Art; and letters from Hanes to Castle, February 10, 1969, and January 15, 1970, Castle Papers, Archives of American Art. See also *Newsweek* 1968.

29. A laminated and painted stool by Castle is listed in Seattle 1968, 12, and a *Double Elephant Table* of gold-painted wood is in Wichita 1969, no. 5.

30. See Wichita 1969, nos. 6, 7, 17.

31. On the fundamental distinctions between the work of Castle and Krenov and their respective approaches to teaching, see Bertorelli 1983.

32. Letter from Nordness to Castle, April 9, 1970, Nordness Papers, Archives of American Art.

33. Castle's one-person exhibition at the Memorial Art Gallery in 1965 included several sketches for gazebos. Although Baker, an art director and owner of a Rochester advertising agency, expressed interest in these, he did not decide to ask Castle to realize one until his Castle-designed table developed problems. Fearful that Castle could not create a comparable replacement, Baker commissioned him to create a gazebo in 1972.

34. Among the commissions that Johnson gave Castle in the early 1970s, the most significant was the one for the stair. Since it was the first stair he had ever designed, it presented several new kinds of problems. Castle wrote to Johnson: "The staircase has been quite a challenge, but I finally have it all figured out and I am happy with the result. It is a major piece which involves solving technical problems as well as aesthetic ones. I have managed to arrange my work schedule for the next four months to devote almost full-time to your projects. Some of my present customers do not mind waiting a little extra time and I have hired one more additional craftsman" (letter from Castle to Mr. and Mrs. Samuel C. Johnson, July 19, 1972, Castle Papers, Archives of American Art).

35. Preliminary drawings for this sculpture are in the Castle Archives, Scottsville, New York.

36. El-Zoghby 1970, 13.

37. As part of a marketing campaign, Castle developed a brochure highlighting his work as "provocative—yet practical." The brochure stated that the formation of Wendell Castle Associates would make the plastic and wood furniture of "this gifted designer and craftsman" available to the broader public, especially architects and interior designers. A copy of this brochure is in the object folder for Castle's *Two-Seater* (1979), Department of American Decorative Arts and Sculpture, Museum of Fine Arts, Boston.

38. Wendell Castle Associates 1973.

39. On the emergence of art furniture in the twentieth century and the role of Surrealists like Meret Oppenheim, Dali, and René Magritte in creating furniture that dissolved the boundaries between the fine and the decorative arts, see Philadelphia, University of Pennsylvania, Institute of Contemporary Art,

Improbable Furniture (1977); on Italian postwar plastic furniture design in general and its impact on America, see DiNoto 1984. DiNoto discusses the relationships among Dali's sofa (based on Mae West's lips), Studio 65's version for Gufram, and Castle's Molar group (see figs. 269–271).

40. It is interesting to note that the illustrations and the rhetoric in the brochure for these signed pieces emphasize the handwork involved in the production of laminated pieces. A copy of this brochure can also be found in the files of the Museum of Fine Arts, Boston (see note 37, above).

41. Jonathan Fairbanks, curator of American decorative arts and sculpture at the Museum of Fine Arts, began a gallery seating program entitled "Please Be Seated" in 1976. By matching National Endowment for the Arts Museum Purchase funds with corporate or foundation support, Fairbanks commissioned contemporary furniture makers to make public seating for the permanent collection. Sam Maloof made fourteen pieces in 1976, and Castle, George Nakashima, Tage Frid, and Judy McKie each made pieces in 1979.

42. Russell 1978, 32.

43. See Hunter-Stiebel 1979/80.

44. All of these chairs display close ties to the work of twentieth-century industrial designers. The *Zephyr Chair*, for instance, is a wooden version of Hans and Wassili Luckhardt's 1931 tubular-steel chair; see Derek E. Ostergard, ed., *Bentwood and Metal Furniture: 1850–1946* (New York: American Federation of Arts, 1987), 135, 294–295.

45. Growing public awareness of contemporary craft and a concern for the role of the craftsman in society prompted several symposia on these topics, including a two-day seminar on "Employment of the Craftsman" organized in conjunction with the exhibition "New York State Craftsmen: 1972 Selections," held in March and April 1972 at the State University of New York at Albany.

46. Letter from Fendrick to Castle, September 25, 1980, Fendrick Gallery Archives, Washington, D.C.

47. Meilach 1975.

48. Esherick first used the three-sided table shape in a 1947 hickory cocktail table, but he continued to use it in the 1950s and 1960s; see *Craft Horizons* 17 (March/April 1957): 37; Castle 1970, 15; and Stone 1986, 17.

49. For a general discussion of the illusionistic sculpture movement in America during the late 1960s and early 1970s, see Kim Levin, "The Ersatz Object," *Arts Magazine* 58 (March 1984): 88–91; and Lucie-Smith 1980, 51–63. The chapter in Lucie-Smith's book is particularly significant since he discusses the illusionism of contemporary ceramics, furniture, and jewelry within the context of 1970s trompe l'oeil painting and sculpture.

50. Edgar 1978, 37.

51. Kagan showed illusionistic works by Castle in his 1979 shows "Hardwood Furniture and Objects: Fall '79" and "More Wood: An Exhibition of Smaller Pieces," and again in 1981 in "The Growth of a Tradition: Fifteen Woodworkers." Barbara Fendrick also included examples of this work in her 1978 and 1980 "Furniture as Art" exhibitions.

52. The exhibition included two other works by Castle: *Three-Legged Desk*, 1977, maple, walnut, and zebrawood, and *Leather-Topped Desk*, ca. 1978, stack-laminated maple and leather.

53. Yoskowitz 1981.

54. Russell 1981.

55. For information on Makepeace's school, see Castle 1979.

56. Among the graduates of Castle's school are well-known studio furniture makers Wendy Stayman and Peter Pierobon, designer Michael Scott, and commercial furniture makers David Doernberg and John Zanetti.

57. Lucie-Smith 1980.

58. Waller knew Castle's work well since, first as curator and then director of the University of Kansas Museum of Art, he had arranged for Castle's 1969 one-person exhibition to be shown there.

59. Quoted in Rochester 1981a, 6.

60. Letter from Baker to Milliken, February 3, 1982, Alexander F. Milliken, Inc., Archives, New York.

61. Quoted in *Fine Woodworking* 1981.

62. Spearheaded by collector and gallery owner Holly Solomon, the Pattern and Decoration movement began in the mid-1970s and involved work in all media that focused on the physical properties of an object, particularly its shape, surface texture, color, and size. The work of artists Robert Kushner, Joyce Kozloff,

Kim MacConnel, Miriam Schapiro, Betty Woodman, Brad Davis, and Thomas Lanigan-Schmidt is most closely associated with this movement. Since many of these artists chose to decorate utilitarian objects, their work, often referred to as "usable art," challenged the existence of barriers between the fine and the decorative arts. For a general discussion of the movement, see Miami, the Museum of the American Foundation for the Arts, *Patterning and Decoration* (1977); and Plattsburgh, New York, Myers Fine Arts Gallery, *Usable Art* (1981). See also Jensen and Conway 1983, which provides a good visual compendium of the work of artists associated with the movement and briefly discusses Castle's trompe l'oeil works and fine furniture.

63. Lucie-Smith 1979, 206.

64. See Plakins 1983 and Kelsey 1983.

65. In 1983 Castle established an arrangement with Arc International whereby he would design prototypes for a furniture line that would be fabricated by a subcontractor under Castle's auspices, then distributed and marketed by Arc. See letter from Joseph Z. Duke, president of Arc International, to Castle, May 19, 1983; letter from William Grenewald, vice-president of Arc International, to Castle, May 7, 1984; and letter from Castle to Grenewald, May 5, 1985, Castle Archives, Scottsville, New York.

66. See Castle 1969.

67. For more on plate joinery, see Paul Bertorelli, "Plate Joinery," *Fine Woodworking* 34 (May/June 1982): 95–97.

68. Some of the clocks were included in the exhibition "Masterpieces of Time," which opened at the Taft Museum in Cincinnati in 1985 and circulated, with modifications, in 1985–86 to Alexander F. Milliken, Inc., in New York and the Renwick Gallery in Washington, D.C. Several were also exhibited in "Time and Defiance of Gravity: Recent Works of Wendell Castle," which was organized by the Memorial Art Gallery of the University of Rochester in 1986 and subsequently traveled to the Mead Art Museum at Amherst College, Amherst, Massachusetts.

69. Brown 1985a.

70. Holmes 1986.

71. Chastain-Chapman 1986.

72. For an illustration of Esherick's desk, see Stone 1986, 12–13.

73. The most important exhibition of the 1970s documenting the art-furniture movement was "Improbable Furniture," organized by the Institute of Contemporary Art at the University of Pennsylvania, Philadelphia (catalogue by Suzanne Delahanty and Robert Pincus-Witten), March 10–April 10, 1977. Other significant exhibitions include: New York, Marian Goodman Gallery, "Further Furniture," December 1980; Providence, Rhode Island, Rhode Island School of Design, "Furniture Furnishings: Subject and Object," March 16–June 27, 1984; Newport Beach, California, Newport Harbor Art Museum, "Future Furniture," 1985; and Indianapolis, Center for Contemporary Arts, Herron Gallery, "The Furniture Show: Contemporary Lamps, Tables by Furniture Makers/Artists," January 24–March 7, 1987 (which included work by Castle). Perhaps the most cogent recent statement on the movement was written by Mary Jane Jacob for the 1987 exhibition "The Eloquent Object," organized by the Philbrook Museum of Art in Tulsa (which also included work by Castle).

74. Domergue 1984.

75. Quoted in Forsman 1986.

76. The input of Pierobon was particularly important in this body of work in terms of the use of the zigzag form and the emphasis on fantasy.

77. One of the most lucid reviews of the new work was written by Jo Ann Lewis in response to the Fendrick Gallery's 1986 exhibition "Wendell Castle: Sculpture? Furniture? The Vanishing Line." See Lewis 1986.

78. The Philadelphia Museum of Art and the Art Institute of Chicago are two institutions that have recently added to their holdings of Castle's work.

79. Castle initially designed the paneling of Joseph's room to resemble that of Milliken's. See preliminary drawings for the Joseph room in the Castle Archives, Scottsville, New York.

80. The projects not discussed in this essay are furnishings for the foyer of the Cincinnati Art Museum (completed in 1988) and the *Tick-Tock Kick Clock* for the interior of the DuPont Centre in Orlando, Florida (installed in 1987).

81. Conversation, Davira S. Taragin with Castle, July 1988.

Plate 42
Lady's Desk with Two Chairs, 1981
(checklist no. 23)

105

been limited to sculpture. He has since crossed over into Post-Modernist architectural forms, into design, and most recently into painted sculpture.

What is salient about Castle is that having broken down the barriers between established categories he stays in the in-between. It is a position characteristic of much recent art, craft, design, decorative arts, and architecture, and one with many ramifications for contemporary art history.

The characterization of art as nonfunctional is, historically, a relatively recent assumption, one that has caused considerable controversy. The critic Helen Giambruni wrote in 1987:

> That such a distinction should persist in the anti-aristocratic United States is astonishing, and discouraging. All the more so because this attitude is maintained in the face of what is now universal recognition of the aesthetic significance of functional objects in other societies—say, Shang ceremonial bronzes, Sepik River masks, Byzantine reliquaries, Andean textiles, Minoan jugs, Zen tea cups or Haida oil containers. Is it because these objects have no functional purpose for *us* that we can afford them the dignity of art?[7]

Artists are again straightforward about creating functional art. "Art used to have a function, such as a religious function," said artist Nancy Holt in 1986. "Michelangelo's ceiling is an integral part of its environment, and it was made to be that way. But with modernism, art was stripped of its context and its function. We are putting a function back into art."[8]

For centuries, frescoes, painting, and sculpture were didactic as well as visually engaging—a form of the Bible for the illiterate in churches, and a form of decoration and amusement in houses. The English architectural historian William Curtis has argued that many works of art now exhibited in museums served as a type of furniture in their original settings.[9] When, in the wake of Europe's wars, great estates were broken up, furnishings that had for centuries occupied the same spaces were separated from one another for the first time and relegated to museums of either fine or decorative arts, depending on whether they were considered functional or nonfunctional—a distinction that had been developing for some time. "By 1849, the modern distinction between artist and artisan (and therefore between art for beauty and craft for use) was fixed in the English language," writes Brent Brolin in *Flight of Fancy*. He goes on to cite the nineteenth-century French writer Théophile Gautier's reasoning about the nature of useful objects: "Nothing is really beautiful unless it is useless; everything useful is ugly, for it expresses a need, and the needs of men are ignoble and disgusting, like his poor weak nature."[10] That industrialization removed the hand from the fabrication of everyday objects confirmed the distinction. But the cleft between art and the design arts (industrial design, decorative arts, architecture) may have been wedged most deeply in this century because of the advent of abstraction in the fine arts. Artists pursued visions in which use was simply not a subject.

Still, there have always been institutions and individuals who resisted the split. The Arts and Crafts movement, in its various incarnations, narrowed the gap by minimizing the presence of the machine and revaluing the hand. In America, Louis Comfort Tiffany created works that, in the aesthetic of the time, blurred the boundaries between the artistic and the useful, as did Josef Hoffmann of the Wiener Werkstätte and the Scottish designer and architect Charles Rennie Mackintosh. Various modernist artists and institutions also opposed the division. The Bauhaus was founded to integrate artists into its design programs and processes, proclaiming in its *Manifesto* (1919), "There is no essential difference between the artist and the craftsman."[11] The De Stijl architect and cabinetmaker Gerrit Rietveld created, as critic Lynne Cooke describes his *Red-Blue Chair* (fig. 23), "sculpture as furniture/furniture that functions equally as sculpture. . . . Its ability to be viewed as sculpture depends in part on the feeling that it is not immediately inviting to use: it does not promise to be comfortable whereas its proportions and formal balance are an immediate delight to the eye and mind."[12] Then there were artists' comments on the distinction, from Marcel Duchamp's signed urinal to a surrealistic, dysfunctional teacup, saucer, and spoon that were lined with fur in 1936 by Meret Oppenheim (fig. 24). Pablo Picasso and Constantin Brancusi both created art that was furniture. Isamu Noguchi developed several biomorphic designs for furniture intended for the mass market.

But these independent efforts were not sufficient to counter significantly the reigning industrial culture and heal the breach between useful and nonfunctional objects. Several interdependent trends developed after World War II, however, that would give Castle's trompe l'oeil and fancy furniture pieces a resonant context.

American crafts before World War II existed, generally, in their own self-contained worlds, with histories and traditions often based in the vernacular or in foreign cultures. Potters, for example, looked to Japan; Appalachian wood craftsmen made objects from materials at hand because they needed them and did so in expedient ways that grew out of

Figure 23
Gerrit Rietveld, Dutch, 1888–1964, *Red-Blue Chair*, executed by G. Van de Groenekan, 1950s, based on original design of 1918. Courtesy of Barry Friedman, Ltd., New York.

Figure 24
Meret Oppenheim, Swiss, 1913–1985, *Object (Fur-Covered Cup, Saucer, and Spoon)*, 1936. New York, The Museum of Modern Art, Purchase.

local traditions. After the war, however, with many GIs enrolled in college, students typically studied crafts in art schools or the fine-arts departments of universities, where they encountered the same ideas as other art students. Programs included furniture making, weaving, ceramics, glassmaking, and other crafts. As Giambruni described it:

> The result, of course, was an explosion of creativity in fine arts–oriented crafts that began in the late 1950s and early 1960s. It was an intoxicating period of emancipation where a ceramicist or weaver or glassmaker could push aside the traditional restraints of function, accumulated skills and craft history, and respond freely to the most challenging currents in contemporary art.[13]

The result was the start of a new tradition in the crafts that has come to be known as the Studio Craft movement. Giambruni wrote: "In effect, it was the academicians who helped raise crafts to an art. Products of college courses, these same craft artists were then hired to teach their craft. Freed from the necessity of selling their wares to exist, they began to focus on exhibition objects."[14] Strong support for this changing outlook within the crafts came in the 1960s from the American Craftsmen's Council's magazine *Craft Horizons*, whose editor-in-chief Rose Slivka had what has been described as openness to the new and passion for art.

The break with function first occurred in clay. Beginning in the 1950s Peter Voulkos applied principles of Abstract Expressionism to clay sculpture, creating colorful, distorted forms far from the traditional image of the pot (see fig. 25). In glass Harvey Littleton pushed the medium to new limits with sculptural arcs and loops resembling rainbows. Lenore Tawney and Claire Zeisler wove fabrics in multiple planes to create a three-dimensional sense of space. In the 1960s Castle himself laminated woods into blocks that he carved into highly sculptural free-form shapes, which carried a strong message: in the ethos of the time, they were protests against the values of the dominant industrial culture. Anthony Urbane Chastain-Chapman wrote of Castle:

> Against this background of sculpture and furniture styles that emphasized industrial technology and denied craftsmanship, the natural carved forms, oiled woods and careful craftsmanship of Castle's 1960s work should be seen as a reaction, a form of protest in tune with the social climate of that decade. This timeliness perhaps accounts for the ready response to Castle's early work, and for its widespread influence on woodworkers. Noguchi's biomorphic furniture forms in the 1940s had been merely novel; Castle's, in the 1960s, were relevant.[15]

Other artists were quick to accept this new point of view, as critic Katherine Pearson writes: "Each of these innovators, each in his respective discipline, has influenced a whole new generation of artists. Working in craft media, they are bridging the Oriental respect for materials and craftsmanship with the American aggressive urge for self-expression."[16]

When Castle showed his work, freighted with an artistic agenda and substantial price tags, at a prestigious fine-arts gallery in New York, this whole phenomenon of crafted art came into focus. For the crafts a shift toward "art" was radical in fundamental ways: the

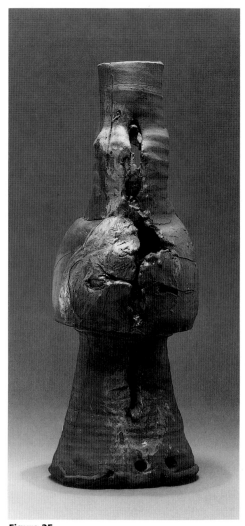

Figure 25
Peter Voulkos, American, born 1924, *Untitled Stack Pot*, 1964. Detroit Institute of Arts, Founders Society Purchase, Miscellaneous Memorials Fund (1985.28).

Figure 26
Richard Artschwager, American, born 1924, *Description of Table*, 1964. New York, Whitney Museum of American Art, Gift of the Howard and Jean Lipman Foundation, Inc. (66.48).

visual presence of a piece now outweighed its function, design outweighed technique, and form was more important than material. But at the same time as craft was becoming art, the fine-arts and design worlds were shifting in similarly fundamental ways. Artists and designers were beginning to create works that occupy the same blur.

If the nature of the avant-garde had been to shock, artists—after Andy Warhol's soup cans, Jasper Johns's American flags, Carl André's bricks, Christo's wrappings—have lost that ability: the audience has been shocked out. Artists can, however, expand the notion of just what the boundaries of art are, and one way of doing this is to extend art into the areas of design and functionalism, pattern and decoration, advertisement and commercial art. Many works created in this changed environment blur these previously separate categories. The blurring helps to demystify art—you can now sit on it or decorate with it—although it becomes increasingly difficult and inappropriate to define. Categories seem to dissolve, leaving the object standing alone.

A seminal figure who has created many images of furniture—and with whose work Castle was familiar in the 1960s—is Richard Artschwager. A wood craftsman turned artist, Artschwager in the early 1960s "painted" real furniture into unusability and crafted sculptures in plastic laminate that were configured and surfaced to represent furniture. His *Description of Table* of 1964 (fig. 26), a cube laminated in Formica to represent a table with a white tablecloth, prefigures by more than twenty years a traveling show entitled "Material Evidence," consisting of works created by craftsmen in Formica's Colorcore laminate.[17]

Artschwager's pieces, of course, only represent furniture and are not intended to be usable, but they nevertheless established the blur that others were profitably to occupy, explore, and exploit. His "furniture" pieces allude to the human figure and to function, but they are also abstract: Artschwager put familiar forms in a new context and expanded the conceptual framework within which art has operated. In his painted pieces and his pieces "drawn" in Formica, there is a blur between painting and sculpture as well as between art and furniture.

Other artists, coming from widely varying backgrounds, also turned to furniture. Donald Judd's minimal abstractions exhibit a strong, direct presence: it is the materiality of the work that matters most, not whether or not it is a table. Robert Rauschenberg, Lucas Samaras, Robert Morris, and Alan Siegel all work in furniture. But it is Scott Burton who, starting with his *Bronze Chair* (1972/75), consistently makes sculpture that is usable, situating his work between art and design. The bronze chair, which originated in a performance tableau, is nothing more than, in Burton's words, a bronzed "Grand Rapids Queen Anne," and as is true of Castle's wooden chair (without the crushed hat), only an inversion of expectations keeps it from becoming a seat. Burton's piece does not lose its identity as a functional object, but it refuses to "take sides" and thus resolve its inherent ambiguity. Burton sustains this ambiguity throughout his work. Anyone coming across his rock chair in the garden of the Museum of Modern Art in New York, carved with a few cuts from live rock, is caught between wanting to look and wanting to sit.

Beyond the blur between art and furniture is the broader blur between art and design. Burton, a Minimalist who introduces conventional furniture functions into otherwise neutral blocks, eschews any personal expression. "I think the only way out is to imitate the design arts, where your personality is not the most important thing," he has said.[18] Increasingly for Burton, freedom from artistic precedents is not of major importance. Burton and Castle are, in this respect, diametrically opposed. Burton's crisp, cool works, most recently done in stone, have few associations; Castle's pieces are redolent with associations, depending on the period: biomorphic, trompe l'oeil, fine furniture, Post-Modern architecture, painterly sculpture. Castle saturates his work with associations that allude to sources outside craft. Still, Castle's work, like Burton's, occupies an ambiguity that tenses the work.

Not all artists working with furniture develop the junctions between categories as deliberately as Burton. Some simply need a chair or table and improvise one. But whether as a deliberate or casual effort, "virtually every artist working in the 1970s has done one or several pieces based on the furniture theme, ranging from a miniature chair by Joel Shapiro to the *Dinner Party* by Judy Chicago," observes curator Charles F. Stuckey.[19]

Two other major trends have resulted in activity in the blur between art and furniture. In 1981, at the Milan Furniture Fair, the angular neo-Pop furniture in acid colors by MEMPHIS MILANO (fig. 27) made its first appearance, a spectacular introduction that seemed to spring full-blown from the head of the group's leader, Ettore Sottsass. The furniture is intended to be manufactured—they are not one-of-a-kind, made-by-hand pieces—but the designs still

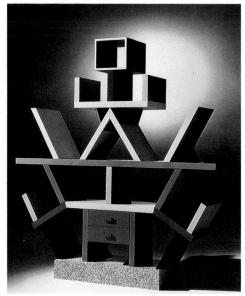

Figure 27
Ettore Sottsass, Italian, born 1917, *Carlton Room Divider*, 1981, designed for MEMPHIS MILANO. Courtesy of Urban Architecture, Inc., Detroit.

subvert "design" by subordinating function to appearance and meaning. The MEMPHIS group juxtaposes expensive marbles and kitchen-counter laminates, devaluing the one, revaluing the other, without too many ergonomic considerations. The visual presence of the furniture dominates its nominal function.

The second trend is the sweeping art-furniture movement of the 1970s and 1980s.[20] Lynne Cooke describes much of this work as

> neither a sideline nor an occasional byproduct, but the chief concern of the sculptors, most of whom come from fine arts backgrounds and operate exclusively within this realm. Some works tend to be assertively individualistic and so take on the aura and uniqueness peculiar to sculpture rather than the qualities of a mass-produced artefact, so intricate the crafting, so expensive the materials, and so rebarbarative to use their form.[21]

There are many strains in the movement, but one of the most consciously cultivated has been the effort to mix art and design so that art is no longer fashioned solely in its own image; it becomes less self-referent and draws on the applied and decorative arts. "What has changed is seeing design as a potential art form—designers now see themselves in a different way," observes Rick Kaufmann, head of Art et Industrie, a Manhattan gallery that has helped catalyze the movement. He has encouraged work, he says, that is not design about art, like the works of MEMPHIS, or art about design, like that of Burton or Artschwager.[22] Forrest Myers, one of the artists who shows at Art et Industrie, says, "We're trying to get furniture to transcend itself, to become something on a higher plane—a work of art."[23] Conversely, "although Burton is frequently thought of as a maker of 'art furniture,' the classification is imprecise," writes critic Patricia C. Phillips. " 'Art furniture' is conceived as furniture with aspirations toward art, while Burton's pieces are conceived as art that becomes furniture. It is a dramatically different sensibility."[24]

Dan Friedman, a graphic designer turned furniture artist (see fig. 28) who has shown at Art et Industrie, has said:

> The boundary lines between design, craft, and art, that's what I've been sitting on for a number of years. It comes from a feeling that there's a need for a personal, human-scale artistic expression. As a designer, I feel that objects that the art world has created have been too anonymous; so much of what you find is done for museums. Instead of the limitation that form follows function, I came to believe that form can embody other aspects of our existence, including fantasy, and still function. From my point of view, it's more general than [the issue of] the painted surface—[it is] a return to craftsmanship and personal statements made with hands.[25]

Occupation of the blur has not been confined to the small object. One of the most original figures in contemporary architecture, Frank Gehry, has absorbed many lessons from artists—drawing upon illusionism, light-and-shadow painting, the use of scrims, even exposed-stud construction—and produced what might be called the ultimate pieces of art furniture: buildings. He has said, "I approach something just like Oldenburg—I think about

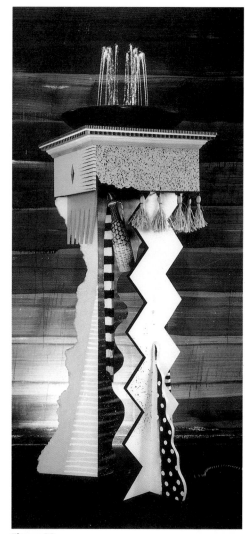

Figure 28
Dan Friedman, American, *Fountain of Youth*, 1985. Courtesy of Art et Industrie, New York.

Figure 29
Frank Gehry, American, born 1929, *Experimental Edges Rocker*, 1980. Collection of the architect. Photo courtesy of the Walker Art Center, Minneapolis.

materials, I think about context, and about materials in context." The results are so "artistic" that he frequently has to assert: "I'm not an artist, I'm an architect." Referring to his own cardboard furniture (see fig. 29), he has said, "I'm not a furniture designer, I'm an architect."[26]

The blur seems to be occurring at every possible junction, between art, craft, design, decorative arts, and architecture, crossovers that purposely never make it to the other side. The blur may be occurring in the context of a larger phenomenon within postindustrial culture, where the promise of the machine to deliver higher standards of living has been replaced by the promise of art to foster greater personal fulfillment. Museums rather than churches are being built in the downtowns of American cities, and they project the sense that art has become the central concern, purpose, subject, and pleasure of the culture.

A phenomenon that started in the 1960s and 1970s with several notable figures, including Castle, came to a boiling point by the mid-1980s, precipitating a crisis of judgment: how are these pieces to be evaluated? To splice categories and cultivate the blur was, perhaps, an original statement in itself, but some crossovers have amounted to a kind of miscegenation. Lynne Cooke, writing about Burton and "the current fashion for furniture sculpture," says the fashion "owes much to his [Burton's] example even as it betrays and misunderstands his ideals and achievement."[27] Burton himself has strong reactions to the deluge. While he may have the highest regard for Donald Judd's work in furniture—"His preoccupations seem to integrate seamlessly with his [furniture] designs; his work has rigor"[28]—

Burton labels the work of many others "corrupt and commercial . . . done by failing artists turning to furniture."[29]

Crossover pieces require multiple criteria of judgment—they have to be seen as craft, art, and design simultaneously, as both functional and nonfunctional. There should be a reason to occupy the blur; the crossover should resonate from both sides. Castle's trompe l'oeil pieces succeed, for instance, because the visual illusion depends on the high quality of the craft; the illusion, in turn, transforms the concept of craft and furniture. To maintain the tension of two disciplines cohabiting a single piece, the artist should not erase the categories but straddle them. The crossover work is more a hybrid than a synthesis; the vigor comes from the interplay. When this tension is lacking, the work becomes simply one thing trying to be another. As Cooke writes:

> The arch artiness and promiscuous eclecticism in Christopher Sproat's furniture is typical of the way in which this type of work ultimately seeks the glamour and role of sculpture, its involvement with the problems of furniture largely specious and frivolous. More interesting is the work of Siah Armajani which seeks to play the two modes off against each other in more searching fashion.[30]

Elsewhere in the same article, Cooke says, "In the seventies Burton walked a tightrope between these two areas, avoiding the gravest danger of all, that of invoking one art form superficially or nominally in the service of the other."[31] Calvin Tomkins, writing about artists redefining art, says: "A straining after effect is apparent in much of the work in other media, as though the maker, uneasily astride the tightrope between craft and art, has confused cleverness with imagination. There is neither the serenity of traditional craftwork nor the authority of an artistic statement."[32]

Castle himself occupies territory with a very wide blur, but the blurring in Castle's work has a long, complicated history. Castle's forte has been his workmanship, a fact that Castle has recognized:

> I'd always read that the eighteenth century was the high point in the history of furniture, but it meant nothing to me until I saw a lot of that furniture. It was spectacular stuff. And it confirmed what I'd read about people like Ruhlmann wanting to return to the principles of the eighteenth century. I discovered that workmanship was more important than I'd previously given it credit for being. I'd always thought that it would detract from the art. In lesser hands, when technique outshines the form and idea, I still think it does. But in the hands of someone capable of handling it, workmanship becomes an incredible, awesome thing. It's almost an art in itself, although a lot of the art is invisible. Now there are a lot of elements in my work that don't show.[33]

But some critics feel Castle's forays into the blur have led him to create works that betray the craft: the concept is not the equal of the workmanship, and the disparity is all the more glaring because the "design" is flamboyant. In her review of the inaugural show at the

American Craft Museum's new Fifty-third Street building, "Craft Today: Poetry of the Physical," Giambruni discussed those who

> operate on the principle of the more forced and contorted, the better. The discipline and restraint imposed by function would have helped a lot in such cases. I will cite only one piece in illustration here, and not because it is anything like the worst but because Wendell Castle offers a big target. Castle and his workshop produce pieces of extraordinary technical virtuosity and the "Ziggurat Clock" in the show is no exception. But it strives too hard for sculptural effect and ends up grandiose and bombastic.[34]

Although some of his work visibly "brags" about its craftedness, Castle seldom makes gratuitous displays of technique. Lately his work has in fact headed in the opposite direction: he has been making quizzical, quasi-organic furniture in distorted shapes with painted surfaces that subordinate the workmanship. Castle seems to be enlarging the blur between craft and sculpture to include painting, and in doing so he loses the qualities that anchor the best of his work.

The difficulties Castle has encountered by dealing with categorical ambiguities typify the difficulties latent in this ambitious endeavor, the crossover. There are artists who have already abandoned the effort. "The fact that many of these artists are now forsaking this hybrid area . . . attests to the difficulties of answering to two masters simultaneously," writes Cooke.[35] Such artists, who have worked in the blur, are now returning to "purer" categories, believing they should rethink the hierarchies the categories imply: that craft, for example, should maintain its generic distinction from art and develop within its own parameters to achieve aesthetic parity with painting and sculpture.

Still, crossover efforts have, altogether, produced extraordinary results, and what has emerged from the blur—art into design, design into craft, craft into art and design, etc.—is that the "object," whether furniture or sculpture or even architecture, has been defined with such vitality that the "object" has emerged as a category with the generic potential of painting and sculpture. By and large, the new category cannot be described in the critical terms that come out of painting and sculpture. "It's changed things forever," says Kaufmann, owner of Art et Industrie.[36]

If the 1960s was a decade of imagery, and the 1970s of concept, the 1980s has been the decade of the object. Whether functional or not, the new object has not led into what art critic Rosalind Krauss, in a seminal essay, called sculpture in the expanded field,[37] but has, instead, imploded to become an object of great intensity and imagistic density, one with strong visual presence, metaphoric powers, and tactile charisma. The emphatic physicality of these works elicits our interaction. Certainly, the American craft world is now in a place more creative than any in its history due largely to the crossover phenomenon. But this blurring has also greatly heightened creativity in art, design, and architecture. Crossovers based in craft are simply a subset within a much larger, very fecund phenomenon.

1. In conversation with the author, October 1988.
2. Daw 1983, 58. Castle was already represented by the Fendrick Gallery in Washington, D.C.
3. In conversation with the author, October 1988.
4. Russell 1983.
5. In conversation with the author, October 1988.
6. Russell 1983.
7. Giambruni 1987.
8. Quoted in Douglas McGill, "Sculpture Goes Public," *New York Times Magazine* (April 27, 1986).
9. In conversation with the author, early 1970s.
10. Brent Brolin, *Flight of Fancy* (New York: St. Martin's Press, 1985), 72.
11. Quoted in Lucie-Smith 1986, 111.
12. Lynne Cooke, "Scott Burton," *Artscribe International* 51 (December 1985/January 1986).
13. Giambruni 1987, 20.
14. Ibid.
15. Chapman 1983, 69.
16. Katherine Pearson, "Laurels at Last," *American Arts* 12 (July 1981): 31.
17. See New York 1984b.
18. In conversation with the author, ca. 1984.
19. Charles F. Stuckey in the catalogue (p. 9) of the 1983 exhibition "Scott Burton Chairs," co-organized by the Contemporary Arts Center in Cincinnati and the Fort Worth Art Museum.
20. The term "art furniture" was anticipated by the title of two shows at the Fendrick Gallery in Washington, D.C., "Furniture as Art," held in 1978 and 1980.
21. Cooke 1985–86 (note 12, above).
22. In conversation with the author, 1988.
23. In conversation with the author, 1988.
24. Patricia C. Phillips, "Review of Scott Burton Show at Baltimore Museum of Art," *Artforum* 25 (April 1987): 134.
25. In conversation with the author, ca. 1986.
26. In conversation with the author, 1985.
27. Cooke 1985–86 (note 12, above).
28. In conversation with the author, ca. 1984.
29. In conversation with the author, 1988.
30. Cooke 1985–86 (note 12, above).
31. Ibid.
32. Calvin Tomkins, "Erasing the Line," *New Yorker* 56 (July 28, 1980): 87.
33. Quoted in Hemphill 1984, 252.
34. Giambruni 1987, 21.
35. Cooke 1985–86 (note 12, above).
36. In conversation with the author, 1988.
37. Rosalind Krauss, "Sculpture in the Expanded Field," *October*, no. 8 (Spring 1979).

NOTES

The author wishes to thank Scott Burton, Barbara Fendrick, Dan Friedman, Frank Gehry, Rick Kaufmann, Joan Simon Menkes, Alexander F. Milliken, Fran Nelson, Max Protetch, and Paul J. Smith, all of whom provided valuable information in interviews.

In these notes, shortened citations consisting of either the author's name or the periodical/newspaper title plus the date of publication (for books and articles) or city and date (for exhibition catalogues) have been used for items that appear in full form in the Exhibition History and Bibliography sections at the back of this book.

Plate 43
Bench, 1988
(checklist no. 38)

ON COMMISSIONS
Wendell Castle

All but the most successful artists accept commissions as a way of assuring income. The obvious advantage of working without commissions is that you can work without specific requirements, which allows maximum freedom. Nothing would be more wonderful than to make whatever you wish.

I like to make tough work. I sometimes have questioned my directions and goals, which means I change my focus. I even left working with wood for a time in the late 1960s to concentrate on large-scale sculpture and furniture in plastic. I do not like to repeat myself. I like to move on to new things. This approach has made it difficult to develop a consistent market.

Artists have long debated the advantages and disadvantages of accepting commissions for specific works of art. I have never positioned myself in either camp. For me, the acceptability of a particular commission depends on the circumstances—some are acceptable and some are not. I see site-specific public art work and site-specific pieces of furniture as very different entities.

With furniture there is always a strong possibility that its location might change, or it might even be sold. Therefore, I believe that it is a mistake to try to be too specific in accommodating the site or to go too far beyond the norm in solving problems. There have been several times when I have been given requirements that asked too much of a piece or have been asked to create something that depended too much on the environment or had some other very specific requirements. People move, get divorced, die, or decide to sell the work. If the work cannot adjust to these changes, then there will be a problem.

The commissions I have accepted in recent years have offered some exciting possibilities without posing too many specific problems. A clock must tell time; a dining table must accommodate a given number of diners; a bench must seat several people. Such basic requirements leave open plenty of possibilities for artistic expression. The resulting works solve a problem but are not too specific to the site.

There is another side to commissions besides artistic freedom that is seldom spoken of—the economics of a commission. The great advantage of commissions is that they allow projects to be spaced in such a way as to allow some control over cash flow. You know when to expect the next payment. With purely speculative works, sales can be erratic and you never know when a sale may occur.

Commissioned work is rarely as profitable as speculative work. There are many reasons for this sad fact. First, the price of a commissioned work must be established before actual work begins. My work is often very experimental, making accurate estimates all but impossible. I always assume that things will run smoothly, but often they do not. I have yet to have someone give me an open-ended budget. Second, I want things that leave my studio to be perfect. If this means redoing parts to get that perfection, then that is what we do. Third, if a commission carries with it a deadline, that too can add to the cost, since in a workshop situation overtime hours may be required to meet that deadline.

Speculative works have none of these problems. When there are extra costs, these can be added to the price of the piece. Therefore, if a piece is unusually successful, the price can be raised, but if the piece is less successful, the price can be set to cover only its cost. None of these adjustments can be made for a commission. On the positive side, some commissions offer the opportunity to have one's work displayed in a significant public place. This may very well outweigh all the obstacles that arise when dealing with such commissions.

My approach to commissions, as to other works, is concerned with maximum freedom. When designing furniture anything should be possible. Nothing should be taboo. Ideas may come from anywhere and be combined in strange relationships that disregard all tradition—as well as modern conventions. I like to abstract the idea of furniture by rejecting modern stylization in favor of fantasy and suggested metaphors. I believe furniture should be sensuous, tactile, and emotional. Great care must be taken in balancing technique and content. Technique must not come into conflict with ideas, content, and the expressive nature of the piece. I am concerned with risk taking and the layering of ideas.

I will try here to reconstruct how a commission develops and attempt to show how my design process works and also how my studio functions in bringing the piece to reality.

On March 18, 1986, I lectured at the Detroit Institute of Arts. At that time I was introduced to members of one of the museum's support groups—the Art of Poland Associates. Concurrently, Davira S. Taragin, curator of twentieth-century decorative arts and design, was involved with an ongoing project to acquire benches for the museum. These benches would be important additions to the museum's collection and would provide, as well, seating in the galleries. Pieces by various artists and designers, such as Scott Burton and George Nelson, had already been acquired, and after this lecture the Associates decided to commission me to do a bench.

In July 1986 the Founders Society of the Detroit Institute of Arts officially engaged me to do preliminary drawings for a bench, and by December the Art of Poland Associates had agreed to fund the project. My first set of drawings was rejected, and I went back to the drawing board and presented new drawings in January 1987. One of these new concepts was selected, and in April I presented three perspective drawings of this design.

By this time the price needed to be negotiated. That is where Sandy Milliken (whose New York gallery represents my work) came into the picture. I had originally proposed that the bench be made of bronze. Milliken suggested that I consider using wood and a less expensive metal so that the piece would fall within the museum's budgetary requirements.

During the summer months of 1987 the acquisition committee of the museum met and approved the piece for its permanent collection. In October the final contracts were signed, and by November the first payment for the piece arrived and final wood-finish samples were presented for approval.

At about that time, the museum's conservators became concerned with one aspect of the design. Because the legs of the piece would have a hand-painted surface, would there be problems with its upkeep? In February 1988 a final decision regarding the legs was made—a wood with natural color, purpleheart (amaranth), would be used. The piece was delivered to the museum in May 1988 and officially dedicated on June 23, 1988.

What follows is a synopsis of how a design becomes reality. All work begins in my sketchbook. I work with two types of paper: Strathmore 400 in a 5½-by-8½-inch sheet, and a 14-by-17-inch rag layout paper, which is a fairly transparent sheet that allows me to trace and make adjustments in my design without having to redraw the entire piece. I usually draw in perspective from the very beginning in an attempt to make the work look as

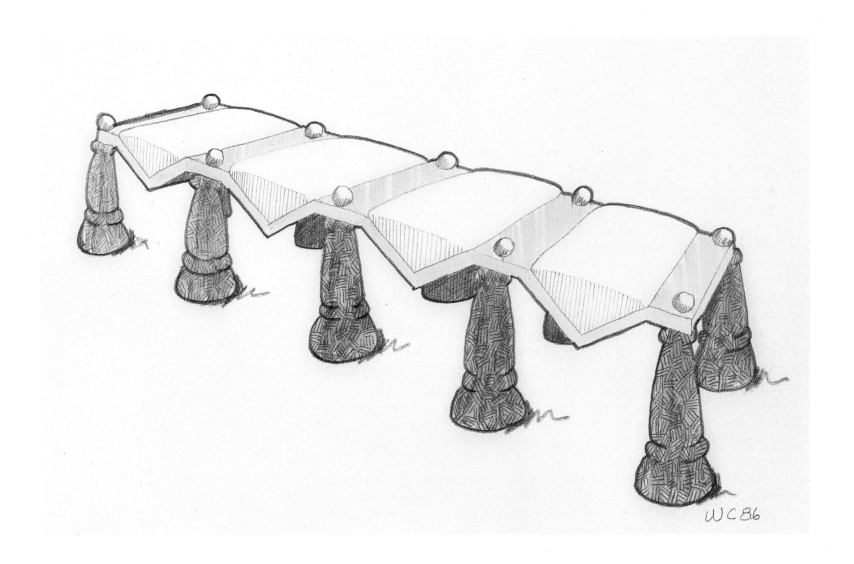

Plate 44
Preliminary proposal for *Bench* project, 1986,
felt marker and pencil on paper, 17.1 × 27.0 cm
(6¾ × 10⅝ in.).

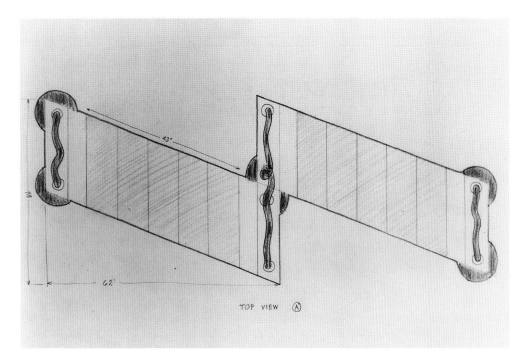

TOP VIEW Ⓐ

Figure 30
Study for *Bench* project, 1987, pencil and colored pencil on paper, 35.2 × 42.9 cm (13⅞ × 16⅞ in.). Detroit Institute of Arts, Founders Society Purchase with funds from the Art of Poland Associates and the Bal Polonais of Detroit (T1987.48).

real as possible. I make no attempt to edit my drawings or to make any decisions as to the merit of any particular design in the early stages of drawing. I try never to erase.

The bench design went through many changes that explored different directions, but a common thread ran through most of the ideas. I wanted to put together several diverse styles and techniques from several different periods of my career. The possibilities included various forms of lamination, natural and painted finishes, geometric forms in wood or metal, variations on texture and color relationships, distortions of scale, etc.

After making a series of sketches over a period of a few months, I narrowed the possibilities down to about six. These designs were redrawn in more accurate perspective and color was added. I then presented these designs for discussion. Some were rejected out of hand. I believe two remained as possibilities, but even some parts of these were under discussion. The final design resulted only after additional work. At this time discussions were also being held concerning the price and selection of materials. Ten months after the project was initiated, we were now ready to begin.

At this point I made full-size drawings so that I could check all relationships and proportions. The resulting measurements were then approved by the museum.

Aluminum was chosen as the material for the zigzag shapes that form the base of the seat. The fabricated aluminum provides structural integrity and in addition creates an excellent interplay in both color and texture with the legs. The zigzag base is not in the shape of a simple rectangle, but rather consists of two rhomboids connected at only one point. The angles of the rhomboids echo those of the zigzags, greatly enhancing the overall composition.

The planning of the pieces and the assembly were quite complex and involved the wonderful skills of several people who work for me. Jim Slowe's engineering background came in handy at this stage. Jim did the working drawings, which identified all the neces-

Figure 31
Final proposal for *Bench* project, 1987, pencil and colored pencil on paper, 35.4 × 43.0 cm (13¹⁵⁄₁₆ × 16¹⁵⁄₁₆ in.). Detroit Institute of Arts, Founders Society Purchase with funds from the Art of Poland Associates and the Bal Polonais of Detroit (1989.25)

sary angles and internal structural considerations. Don Sottile, the studio director, who coordinated the project, consulted with him on these details.

We are not, in the strictest sense, a metal-fabrication shop, but we can handle certain jobs. We cut up all the aluminum parts on a Northfield #4 woodworking saw with a special carbide blade. Bill Schaefer, our welder, was in charge of the fabrication of all the aluminum parts. Bill welded all the components together to achieve the desired forms. Using a Mig welder with the proper wire makes the joints invisible after grinding. Bill also took charge of all the grinding and final finishing, i.e., filling the chamfers on all edges.

I had decided to wait to begin the legs until the zigzag part was complete. This would give me the opportunity to see that everything was in proper relationship, since I could test the legs on the piece at any time. Making the legs was to be my personal contribution to the construction of this piece. Purpleheart is ideal for the bench. The purple color offers great contrast to the aluminum, and the fact that purpleheart is very even in color and texture from board to board helps to obscure the rather complex lamination by which the legs were constructed.

I wanted the legs to seem as if they were a solid form, not a series of boards. The lower leg would be quite straightforward stack lamination with the grain in a vertical direction. The upper part of the leg would be much more complex to construct. This part of the leg would pierce the aluminum (or appear to) and do some twisting and curving and then join the next leg. To accomplish this, I employed stack lamination and a process similar to bricklaying, in which a series of small pieces are stacked together in such a way as to strengthen the joints of the inlaid pieces.

After the lamination process was complete, the forms were carved and rasped to their final shape, then attached to the piece with threaded rods; this allows the legs to be removed, making the piece much easier to transport.

At the same time that I was at work on the legs, Don Sottile was working with Brian Rooney on the leather upholstery. We had chosen black leather since that color works well with the silver-colored metal and the purple wood. The first plan I had for the leather upholstery did not achieve the look I wanted. The first attempt involved stitching a half-round end onto each individual cushion, but the resulting look was not right for the piece, as it was too much like regular upholstery solutions. So we took it all off and started again. Don developed a system of folding the leather back onto itself to create a fan-shaped pattern that works well, giving the work a softer, less formal look. After a total of over six hundred man-hours, the piece was complete and ready to be delivered to the Detroit Institute of Arts.

At any given time, there are probably about six projects going on in the studio. Don and I keep in touch with all of these to make sure that the construction is right and that the look I want is there. It is very exciting in that each day brings about change. I never have the chance to get bored or bogged down with one lengthy, time-consuming project.

The bench for the Detroit Institute of Arts was a particularly rewarding commission, in that I felt I was able to bring to it much of what is important to me in relation to art furniture. Besides being expressive and combining and layering ideas, this bench embodies two additional issues of concern. First, I like to make things that are not what they seem at first glance. In the Detroit bench the relationship between the materials and the form seems jarring and not necessarily harmonious, and even its function may be obscure at first glance. Second, I like to create a sense of delicate balance, to create things that seem to defy gravity. The odd leg arrangement gives the Detroit bench some of this quality. All in all, this piece succeeds on a number of different levels.

Figure 32
Wendell Castle, 1988

1.

Chair, 1958–59
Walnut; nylon
95.3 × 60.3 × 78.7 cm (37½ × 23¾ × 31 in.)
Inscription: none
Collection of Wendell Castle and Nancy Jurs

Exhibition: Lawrence 1959.
Reference: Frazier 1960.
See plate 2.

2.

Stool Sculpture, 1959
Walnut; ivory
154.9 × 59.1 × 94 cm (61 × 23¼ × 37 in.)
Inscription: none
Collection of Wendell Castle and Nancy Jurs

Exhibition: Kansas City 1960.
See plate 4.

3.

Chest of Drawers, 1962
Oak, walnut, birch, oak plywood
120 × 133 × 51.9 cm (47¼ × 52⅜ × 20⁷⁄₁₆ in.)
Inscription: on side of carcass, *WC 62*
Collection of Arlene and Harvey Caplan

Exhibitions: New York 1966.
References: *House Beautiful* 1966, 86; MCC
Annual Report 1966; Page 1966, 115; Castle and
Edman 1980, 148.
See plate 5.

4.

Blanket Chest, 1963
Cherry
91.4 × 86.4 × 33 cm (36 × 34 × 13 in.)
Inscription: on base, *W.C. 63*
Rochester, New York, University of Rochester,
Memorial Art Gallery, Gift of Mr. and Mrs. Michael
L. Watson in memory of Mr. Watson's grandparents

Exhibitions: Rochester 1965; Rochester 1965a;
New York 1966.
References: *Gallery Notes* 1965; *Rochester
Democrat and Chronicle* 1965; *Craft Horizons* 1966,
16; *House Beautiful* 1966, 86; Kelly 1966, 55; *New
Haven Register* 1966; Plumb 1966, 48; *Progressive
Architecture* 1966, 202; Romm 1966; Simpson
1968, 94.
See plate 8.

5.

Rocker, 1963
Walnut; leather
82.6 × 123.2 × 71.8 cm (32½ × 48½ × 28¼ in.)

Inscriptions: on front stretcher, *1963*; on underside
of seat, *W.C.*
Collection of Mr. and Mrs. John Pearsall

Exhibition: Rochester 1964a.
See plate 3.

6.

Music Stand, 1964
Oak, Brazilian rosewood
141 × 63.5 × 50.8 cm (55½ × 25 × 20 in.)
Inscription: underneath lowest slat, *W. C. No. 2/12 64*
New York, American Craft Museum,
Permanent Collection

Exhibitions: Milan 1964; Champaign 1965; Albany
1972; Washington 1972; Milan 1973; Baltimore
1978; New York 1979b; New York 1985; Purchase
1987.
References: Plumb 1964, 117; *Time* 1964, 84; *Life*
1966; Willcox 1968, 66–67; Ketchum 1982;
Hoffman 1985; Brown 1986; Stone 1986, 124.
See plate 6.

7.

Desk and Chair, 1965
Vermilion (padauk)
Desk: 85.1 × 172.7 × 69.9 cm (33½ × 68 × 27½ in.);
chair: 80 × 55.2 × 66 cm (31½ × 21¾ × 26 in.)
Inscriptions: desk, on cavity lid, *W.C. 65*; on
underside of seat, *WC 65*
Collection of Norman S. and Louise R. Levy

Exhibitions: Rochester 1965a; Chicago 1966.
References: Giambruni 1968a, 30; *Rochester
Democrat and Chronicle* 1976.
See plate 10.

8.

Library Sculpture, 1965
Walnut
Stool: 40.3 × 63.3 × 56.8 cm (15⅞ × 24⁵⁄₁₆ × 22⅜ in.);
desk, light, and two connecting chairs:
227.3 × 198.1 × 162.6 cm (89½ × 78 × 64 in.)
Inscriptions: desk, on underside, *W.C. 65*; stool, on
underside of seat, *W.C. 65*
Collection of Mr. and Mrs. Allen Macomber

Exhibitions: Rochester 1965a; New York 1966.
References: McGraw 1965; Braun 1966; *House
Beautiful* 1966, 86; *Interior Design* 1966; McKinley
1966, 42; MCC *Annual Report* 1966; Page 1966,
115; Pahlman 1966; Waldon 1966; Reif 1968;
Simpson 1968, 82; Euaclaire 1977, E: 1.
See plate 1.

CHECKLIST OF THE EXHIBITION

This checklist is arranged chronologically; works
with the same date appear in alphabetical order.
The titles are those under which an object was first
published, or if previously unpublished, the title
preferred by the artist. The date given is normally
the year of completion; a range of years is given
when the exact date is uncertain. Media are cited
in the following order: primary and secondary
woods; veneers; other materials. The identification
of materials is based on information provided by
the artist and on physical examination by the cura-
tors and the staff of the Conservation Services
Laboratory of the Detroit Institute of Arts. Dimensions reflect measurements taken at the widest
point in each direction, with drawers, table leaves,
etc., closed. The References and Exhibitions sections
cite books, catalogues, periodicals, and major
newspaper articles, but no advertisements; nor are
auction catalogues included.

9.

Bookcase, 1967
Oak
193 × 91.4 × 40.6 cm (76 × 36 × 16 in.)
Inscription: on lower left side of carcass, *WC 67*
Belfair, Washington, Lee Nordness Galleries, Inc.

Exhibition: New York 1968.
References: Giambruni 1968; Giambruni 1968a, 31.
See plate 9.

10.

Desk, 1967
Mahogany, cherry plywood; gesso, silver leaf
102.9 × 226.1 × 158.8 cm (40½ × 89 × 62½ in.)
Inscription: on leg near junction with writing
surface, *WC 67*
Racine, Wisconsin, S. C. Johnson & Son, Inc.

Exhibitions: New York 1969; Wichita 1969.
References: Erdle 1968; Giambruni 1968;
Giambruni 1968a, 28; *Newsweek* 1968; Reif
1968a; *Emporia Gazette* 1969; Ashbery 1970, 70;
Feldman 1970; Castle and Edman 1980, 155.
See plate 7.

11.

Benny, 1969
Glass-reinforced polyester, neon
88.3 × 145.4 × 41.9 cm (34¾ × 57¼ × 16½ in.)
Inscription: none
Collection of Wendell Castle and Nancy Jurs

Exhibitions: Rochester 1969; New York 1970;
Buffalo 1971; New York 1972; Toronto 1986.
References: Rogers 1970a; Newman 1974, 114.
See plate 11.

12.

Wall Table No. 16, 1969
Afrormosia
127 × 205.7 × 44.5 cm (50 × 81 × 17½ in.)
Inscription: on base near floor, *WC 69*
Collection of Wendell Castle and Nancy Jurs

Exhibitions: Wichita 1969; New York 1972.
See plate 12.

13.

Molar Chair, 1969–70
Manufactured by Northern Plastics Corporation for
Beylerian Limited
Glass-reinforced polyester
66 × 91.4 × 76.2 cm (26 × 36 × 30 in.)
Inscription: none
Detroit Institute of Arts, Gift of Mr. and Mrs.
Jerome M. Shaw (1987.95)

Exhibitions: Binghamton 1971; Buffalo 1971.
References: Peterson 1971; Reif 1971; Eisenberg
1973; Hill 1975, C: 1; Meilach 1975, 287; DiNoto
1984, pl. 270.
See plate 14.

14.

Executive Desk No. 444, 1974
Cherry, cherry plywood
73.7 × 224.8 × 106.7 cm (29 × 88½ × 42 in.)
Inscription: on lower part of carcass, *WC 74*
Collection of Alan M. Markowitz

Exhibition: Philadelphia 1982.
See plate 41.

15.

Desk, 1977
Maple; zebrawood veneer; walnut inlay
73.6 × 162.6 × 101.6 cm (29 × 64 × 40 in.)
Inscription: on underside, *W.C. 77*
The Brooklyn Museum, Acquisition made possible
through the Louis Comfort Tiffany Foundation

Exhibitions: Washington 1978; New York 1979.
Reference: Heckscher 1981, 15.
See plate 18.

16.

Umbrella Stand, 1977
Maple
90.2 × 33 × 33 cm (35½ × 13 × 13 in.)
Inscription: on exterior near floor, *W.C. 77*
Collection of Peter T. Joseph

Exhibitions: New York 1978; Philadelphia 1978;
Worcester 1978; New York 1979.
On loan: Official residence of the vice-president of
the United States, Washington, D.C., 1979–80.
References: Edgar 1978; Herzig 1978a; Feldkamp
1979; Stapleton 1979/80, 24; Kohen 1980; Lucie-
Smith 1980, 59; Heckscher 1981, 15.
See plate 21.

17.

Chair with Sport Coat, 1978
Maple
92.1 × 47 × 69.2 cm (36¼ × 18½ × 27¼ in.)
Inscription: on lower part of coat, *W. Castle 78*
Collection of Edward J. Minskoff

Exhibitions: New York 1978; Dayton 1980;
Bay Harbor Island 1981.
References: Herzig 1978a; Diamonstein 1983, 33;
Kamm 1983, 24; Stone 1986, 122; *Decorating/
Remodeling* 1988.
See plate 20.

18.

Coatrack with Trench Coat, 1978
Honduras mahogany
190.5 × 58.1 × 54.6 cm (75 × 22⅞ × 21½ in.)
Inscription: on lower part of vertical shaft,
W. Castle 78
Houston, The Museum of Fine Arts, Museum
purchase with funds provided by Roy M.
Huffington, Inc., and anonymous donors

Exhibitions: New York 1978; Washington 1978;
New York 1979; Atlanta 1981.
References: Feldkamp 1979; Kohen 1980;
Heckscher 1981, 15.
See plate 19.

19.

Two-Seater, 1979
Cherry
76.2 × 147.3 × 78.7 cm (30 × 58 × 31 in.)
Inscription: on inner side of support, *W. Castle 79*
Boston, Museum of Fine Arts

Exhibitions: Boston 1978; Boston 1980.
References: Eauclaire 1978a, 60; Fairbanks and
Bates 1981, 521.
See plate 15.

20.

Victory, 1980
Walnut, walnut plywood
71.1 × 175.2 × 91.4 cm (28 × 69 × 36 in.)
Inscription: on base, *W. Castle 80*
Collection of Mr. and Mrs. Norton N. Katz

Exhibitions: Washington 1980; New York 1983b.
References: Conroy 1980; Lewis 1980;
Abercrombie 1982, 78–79; Stone 1986, 119.
See plate 16.

21.

Demilune Table, 1981
Brazilian rosewood, Baltic birch plywood; Brazilian
rosewood veneer; carved ivory, ivory inlay
88.9 × 97.8 × 50.2 cm (35 × 38½ × 19¾ in.)
Inscription: near top of rear leg, *Wendell Castle
1981*
Collection of Mr. and Mrs. Roger Berlind

Exhibition: New York 1983.
References: Abercrombie 1982, 78–79; Bethany
1983; Brayer 1983, B: 1; Chapman 1983, 71;
Davies 1983, 1217; Plumb 1983; Netsky 1984;
Stone 1986, 121; *Woodworker* 1987, 862.
See plate 22.

22.

Egyptian Humidor, 1981
Baltic birch plywood; teak veneer; English sycamore
inlay, Gabon ebony inlay
28.6 × 48.3 × 29.2 cm (11¼ × 19 × 11½ in.)
Inscription: on ebony molding on the back,
Wendell Castle 1981
New York, Alexander F. Milliken, Inc.

Exhibition: New York 1988.
See plate 24.

23.

Lady's Desk with Two Chairs, 1981
Curly English sycamore, purpleheart, ebony, Baltic
birch plywood; curly English sycamore veneer;
ebony inlay, plastic inlay
Desk: 102.5 × 105.4 × 56.5 cm (40⅜ × 41½ × 22¼
in.); chair: 88.2 × 53.3 × 66 cm (34¾ × 21 × 26 in.)
Inscriptions: both chairs, on underside of seat,
Wendell Castle 1981; desk, on underside, *Wendell
Castle 1981*
Collection of Peter T. Joseph

Exhibitions: New York 1981b; New York 1983;
New York 1983c; Cincinnati 1985 (did not travel).
References: *Fine Woodworking* 1981; Abercrombie
1982, 78–79; Andrews 1983, 4; Daw 1983, 58;
Diamonstein 1983, 30, 35; Jensen and Conway
1983, 223; Lovenheim 1983; Plakins 1983, 18;
Hemphill 1984, 244; Findsen 1985; Stone 1986,
123.
See plate 42.

24.

Octagonal-Based Table, 1981
Ebony, Baltic birch plywood; bird's-eye maple
veneer; plastic inlay
72.4 × 83.8 cm (28½ × 33 in.)
Inscriptions: on side of base, *Wendell Castle 1981*;
on underside of base, *Made by W. Castle and
B. Volz*
Los Angeles, Lannan Foundation

Exhibitions: New York 1982; New York 1983.
References: Andrews 1983, 4; *Art Now* 1983,
cover; Brayer 1983, B: 1; Lichtenstein 1983, 49;
Story 1983, 14; Domergue 1984, 62; Netsky 1984;
Russell 1984, C: 9; Stone 1986, 125.
See plate 23.

25.

Table with Gloves and Keys, 1981
Purpleheart
88.9 × 101.6 × 40.6 cm (35 × 40 × 16 in.)
Inscription: on underside, *W. Castle 81*
Collection of Barbara and Thomas Lee

Exhibitions: Chautauqua 1982; Yonkers 1983;
Austin 1985; New York 1988.
See plate 40.

26.

Prototype for Atlantis Desk, 1982
Designed for the Gunlocke Company
Ebonized and lacquered cherry, flakeboard;
beeswing narra veneer; plastic inlay, gold-plated
brass
73.6 × 182.8 × 91.4 cm (29 × 72 × 36 in.)
Inscription: on underside, *W. Castle A/P 1982*
Collection of Kenneth M. Book

Exhibitions: Chicago 1983; Los Angeles 1983;
New York 1983a; Dallas 1984; Houston 1984.
References: Brayer 1983, B: 1; Della Corte 1983,
cover, 131; Giovannini 1983, C: 8; *Interior Design*
1983; Hemphill 1984, 252; Roszkiewicz 1984;
Castle 1986, 87; Stimpson 1987, 174.
See plate 28.

27.

Pleated Bookcase, 1984
Flakeboard; Brazilian rosewood veneer, dyed beech
veneer, curly maple veneer
224.2 × 98.4 × 38.1 cm (88¼ × 38¾ × 15 in.)
Inscriptions: exterior, on carcass at bottom, *Wendell
Castle 1984*; interior, on lower part of door, *Donald
Sottile*
Collection of Mr. and Mrs. Sanford M. Nobel

See plate 27.

28.

Pyramid Coffee Table, 1984
Ebonized cherry, Brazilian rosewood, flakeboard;
Brazilian rosewood veneer; brass
71.1 × 47 × 47 cm (28 × 18½ × 18½ in.)
Inscription: on lower side of pyramid, *Wendell
Castle 1984*
Collection of John French

Reference: Stone 1986, 117.
See plate 26.

29.

Temple Desk and Chair, 1984
Desk: ebonized cherry, Osage orange, ebony,
flakeboard; ebonized imbuya veneer; 23k gold-
plated brass rings
97.8 × 106.7 × 55.9 cm (38½ × 42 × 22 in.)
Chair: ebonized cherry, flakeboard; ebonized
imbuya veneer; Persian lamb upholstery, 23k gold-
plated brass rings
81.3 × 48.3 × 48.3 cm (32 × 19 × 19 in.)
Inscriptions: desk, on drop front, *Wendell Castle
1984*; on lower recessed side, *MADE BY PETER
PIEROBON—W. Castle*; chair, on underside of seat,
Wendell Castle 1984
New York, Alexander F. Milliken, Inc.

Exhibitions: New York 1984c; Austin 1985;
Cincinnati 1985 (did not travel); New York 1988.
References: McCombie 1985; Shukalo 1985;
Berman 1986, 198.
See plate 25.

30.

Ghost, 1985
Mahogany, bleached mahogany
222.3 × 62.2 × 38.1 cm (87½ × 24½ × 15 in.)
Inscription: on bottom of sheet, *Wendell Castle
1985*
New York, Alexander F. Milliken, Inc.

Exhibitions: Cincinnati 1985 (New York and
Washington venues only); Rochester 1986.
References: Gimelson 1985, 102; Hammel 1985a;
Jacobson 1985, C: 1; Kessler 1985; Robinson 1985,
B: 1; Schaire 1985, 69; *Antiques and Arts Weekly*
1986; Byers and Rosenfeld 1986, 2; Chastain-
Chapman 1986, 20; Conroy 1986; Henry 1986;
Holmes 1986, 81; Mayer 1986; Netsky 1986a, C: 8;
New York 1986b, 39; Pearlman 1986, 63; *TWA
Ambassador* 1986; Voell 1986, H: 1; Dormer 1987,
175, fig. 196; Tyler 1987, 47.
See plate 30.

31.

Jester, 1985
Poplar, flakeboard; fiddleback mahogany veneer, imbuya veneer; plastic, gold leaf, leather detailing, ivory detailing
195.5 × 30.5 × 30.5 cm (77 × 12 × 12 in.)
Inscription: on back at bottom, *Wendell Castle 1985*
Collection of Mr. and Mrs. F. Philip Handy

Exhibition: Cincinnati 1985.
References: Brown 1985a, D: 1; *Connoisseur* 1985; *House Beautiful* 1985; Jacobson 1985, C: 1; Robinson 1985, B: 1; Schaire 1985, 68; Allen 1986; *Ambiente* 1986; *Antiques and Arts Weekly* 1986; Bond 1986; Busch 1986, 40; Byers and Rosenfeld 1986, 2; Chastain-Chapman 1986, 21; Conroy 1986; Holmes 1986, 83; Lucie-Smith 1986, 112; Pearlman 1986, 19, 21; Peters 1986; Rochester 1986, 9, 15; *TWA Ambassador* 1986; *Vanidades* 1986; Voell 1986, H: 1; *Washington Uptown Citizen* 1986; *Interior Design Market* 1987; Tyler 1987, 46.
See plate 29.

32.

Never Complain, Never Explain, 1985
Poplar, purpleheart, flakeboard; holly veneer, purpleheart veneer; leather detailing, gold-plated copper rings, plastic inlay, plastic
74.9 × 242.5 × 142.2 cm (29½ × 95½ × 56 in.)
Inscription: on skirt, *Wendell Castle 1985*
Collection of Wendell Castle and Nancy Jurs

Exhibition: Rochester 1986b.
References: Giovannini 1986, C: 10; Netsky 1986.
See plate 31.

33.

Dr. Caligari Desk and Chair, 1986
Desk: painted Yorkite, maple, rosewood, ebonized cherry, flakeboard; rosewood veneer; silver-plated steel pulls
74.9 × 160 × 105.4 cm (29½ × 63 × 41½ in.)
Chair: painted Yorkite, maple, flakeboard
80 × 60.9 × 60.9 cm (31½ × 24 × 24 in.)
Inscriptions: desk, on baseboard, *Wendell Castle 1986*; desk, under top, *Donald Sottile*
Collection of Sydney and Frances Lewis

Exhibition: New York 1986a.
Reference: Busch 1988, 66.
See plate 32.

34.

The Music of Rubber Bands, 1986
Ebonized cherry, lauan plywood; lacewood veneer
96.5 × 162.5 × 55.8 cm (38 × 64 × 22 in.)
Inscription: on upper leg, *Wendell Castle*
New York, Alexander F. Milliken, Inc.

Exhibitions: New York 1986c; Rochester 1986.
Reference: *Fine Arts at Amherst* 1987.
See plate 33.

35.

Untitled (Potted Rubber Tree), 1986
Painted poplar, flakeboard; stained bird's-eye maple veneer; rubber
175.2 × 88.9 × 35.5 cm (69 × 35 × 14 in.)
Inscription: on lower front of cabinet, *Wendell Castle 1986*
Washington, D.C., Fendrick Gallery, Inc.

Exhibition: Washington 1986.
See plate 34.

36.

Humidor, 1987
Painted cherry, flakeboard; stained bird's-eye maple veneer; cedar of Lebanon lining
50.2 × 74.9 × 30.5 cm (19¾ × 29½ × 12 in.)
Inscription: on front rail, *Wendell Castle 1987*
Collection of Mr. and Mrs. William M. Wetsman

See plate 35.

37.

Maquette for Full Moon, 1987–88
Mahogany; aluminum paint, copper, gold-leafed copper
31.4 × 16.5 × 5.1 cm (12⅜ × 6½ × 2 in.)
Inscription: none
Toronto, Hammerson Canada, Inc.

See plate 39.

38.

Bench, 1988
Purpleheart; aluminum, cowhide
88.9 × 329.5 × 121.9 cm (35 × 129¾ × 48 in.)
Inscription: on lower part of middle leg, *Wendell Castle 1988*
Detroit Institute of Arts, Founders Society Purchase with funds from the Art of Poland Associates and the Bal Polonais of Detroit (1988.19)

Reference: Taragin 1989.
See plate 43.

39.

500,000th Commemorative Steinway Piano and Bench, 1988
Piano: mahogany, poplar, maple, Gabon ebony, bubinga, Baltic birch plywood; dyed Swiss pear veneer, East Indian ebony veneer, mahogany veneer; brass
102.2 × 182.6 × 277.8 cm (40¼ × 71⅞ × 109⅜ in.)
Bench: bubinga, Baltic birch plywood; dyed Swiss pear veneer; leather
47 × 88.9 × 41.9 cm (18½ × 35 × 16½ in.)
Inscriptions: piano, on side molding, *Wendell Castle 1988*; bench, on base of leg, *Wendell Castle 1988*
Long Island City, New York, Steinway & Sons (Detroit venue only)

References: *Chicago Tribune* 1987; Jacobson 1987c; *Crafts Report* 1988; Dowling and Solberg 1988; Jacobson 1988d; Jacobson 1988e; Jacobson 1988f; Kimmelman 1988; McShane 1988; Picht 1988; Picket 1988; Rothstein 1988; Sedgewick 1988; Yglesias 1988; *Fine Woodworking* 1989.
See plate 38.

40.

Maquette for Steinway Piano, 1988
Cherry, bubinga, Gabon ebony, flakeboard; East Indian ebony veneer, dyed Swiss pear veneer, mahogany veneer; brass, plastic, tape, paper
32.4 × 55.8 × 91.4 cm (12¾ × 22 × 36 in.)
Inscription: none
Long Island City, New York, Steinway & Sons

See plate 38.

41.

Untitled, 1988
Poplar, Swiss pear; Brazilian rosewood veneer, Swiss pear veneer; leather detailing, gold leaf, silver leaf
289.5 × 121.9 × 121.9 cm (114 × 48 × 48 in.)
Inscription: on base, *Wendell Castle 1988*
Southfield, Michigan, Maccabees Life Insurance Company

References: Benson 1988, 40; Craft 1988.
See plate 37.

1960

Frazier 1960
Frazier, Bernard. "Exhibitions: Kansas Annual." *Craft Horizons* 20 (January/February 1960): 45.

1961

University Daily Kansan 1961
"KU Actress, Fiancé Plan New York Careers." *University Daily Kansan* (March 17, 1961), 10.

1962

Caplan 1962
Caplan, Ralph. "Cross Section, a Personal Look into the Design—and Designed—World: Waste-as-Whimsey." *Industrial Design* 9 (August 1962): 68–70.

Chapman 1962
Chapman, Priscilla. "Crafts Exhibition: Maybe a Shot in the Arm." *New York Herald Tribune* (May 28, 1962).

Home Furnishings Daily 1962
"Young Americans 1962." *Home Furnishings Daily* (May 28, 1962), 1: 10.

House and Garden 1962
"Worth Thinking About." *House and Garden* 122 (October 1962): 164–165.

Interiors 1962
"In the Showrooms—Merchandise Cues: America House Expands Its Facilities to Include More Furniture." *Interiors* 71 (June 1962): 130.

Untracht 1962
Untracht, Oppi. "Young Americans 1962: Enamels, Glass, Wood, Bronze." *Craft Horizons* 22 (July/August 1962): 19–21.

1963

Jones 1963
Jones, Bob. "Art Work on Parade." *University Daily Kansan* (November 7, 1963), 7.

Walrath 1963
Walrath, Jean. "Wood and Metal—Contemporary Sculptures by Two Teachers." *Rochester Democrat and Chronicle* (February 17, 1963), E: 10.

1964

Clune 1964
Clune, Henry W. "Seen and Heard: Crafts and Craftsmen." *Rochester Democrat and Chronicle* (October 4, 1964), M: 4.

Home Furnishings Daily 1964
"Distinctly American." *Home Furnishings Daily* 36 (May 21, 1964).

Indianapolis News 1964
"Hard-to-Get-Gift Is Solomon's." *Indianapolis News* (February 15, 1964), 17.

Plumb 1964
Plumb, Barbara. "New Old Art Nouveau." *New York Times Magazine* (October 11, 1964), 116–119.

Slivka 1964
Slivka, Rose. "The American Craftsman/1964." *Craft Horizons* 24 (May/June 1964): 10–11, 32–33, 112–113, 126.

Smith 1964
Smith, Paul J. "Amusements." *Craft Horizons* 24 (November/December 1964): 9.

Time 1964
"Milan Triennale: Showcase for Good Design." *Time* 84 (September 4, 1964): 83–85.

Walrath 1964
Walrath, Jean. "Exhibitions: 1964 Rochester–Finger Lakes Exhibition." *Craft Horizons* 24 (July/August 1964): 36.

1965

Gallery Notes 1965
Memorial Art Gallery, University of Rochester, New York. *Gallery Notes* 31 (November/December 1965): 3.

McGraw 1965
McGraw, Julie. "Exciting Furniture in Gallery Exhibit." *Rochester Times-Union* (December 16, 1965), C: 10.

Rochester Democrat and Chronicle 1965
"Amateur All at Sea at Lakes Exhibit." *Rochester Democrat and Chronicle* (May 15, 1965), B: 1.

Rochester Times-Union 1965
"RIT Institution Wins Two Art Gallery Prizes." *Rochester Times-Union* (May 15, 1965), A: 8.

1966

Boyen 1966
Boyen, Michael. "Craftsmen USA '66: Northeast Region, Part One." *Craft Horizons* 26 (June 1966): 75–77, 108.

Braun 1966
Braun, Lilian. "Fantastic Furniture, but Usable." *Detroit Free Press* (February 13, 1966), C: 1.

Claremont Vacation-eer, Daily Eagle 1966
"Castle Furniture Exhibit at Hopkins Center." *Claremont [N.H.] Vacation-eer, Daily Eagle* (July 8, 1966).

BIBLIOGRAPHY

Compiled by Jennifer Way with assistance from Melanie Holcomb

Craft Horizons 1966
"Fantasy Furniture." *Craft Horizons* 26 (January/February 1966): 10–17.

Dartmouth Summer News 1966
"'Whimsical' Furniture on Exhibit at Gallery." *Dartmouth [College] Summer News* 4 (July 5, 1966): 1, 4.

House Beautiful 1966
"Rising Stars: Three Designers." *House Beautiful* 108 (January 1966): 86-87.

Interior Design 1966
"Fantasy in Furniture." *Interior Design* 37 (February 1966): 154, 159.

Kelly 1966
Kelly, Scott. "Far-out Furniture." *Industrial Design* 13 (March 1966): 54–57.

Life 1966
"Old Crafts Find New Hands: Weavers, Potters, Workers in Metal, Wood and Glass Reach a High Popularity and Quality." *Life* 61 (July 29, 1966): 34–43.

McKinley 1966
McKinley, Donald. "Exhibitions: Wendell Castle." *Craft Horizons* 26 (March 1966): 41–42.

Maloof 1966
Maloof, Sam. "Wood—A Tape-Recorded Conversation." *Craft Horizons* 26 (June 1966): 16–19.

MCC *Annual Report* 1966
Museum of Contemporary Crafts, New York. *Annual Report* (1966), C.

Minneapolis Tribune 1966
"Fun with Furniture." *Minneapolis Tribune* (April 10, 1966), 31.

New Haven Register 1966
"Far-out Furniture." *New Haven Register* (May 8, 1966).

O'Brien 1966
O'Brien, George. "New Uncrafty Crafts." *Art in America* 54 (May 1966): 69–71.

Page 1966
Page, Marian. "Fantasy Furniture." *Interiors* 125 (February 1966): 113–117.

Pahlman 1966
Pahlman, William. "Fantasy Furniture: An Experience as Well as Household Equipment." *Providence Sunday Journal* (October 9, 1966), F: 14.

Plumb 1966
Plumb, Barbara. "Form Follows Fantasy." *New York Times Magazine* (January 23, 1966), 48–49.

Progressive Architecture 1966
"Furniture as Personal Objects." *Progressive Architecture* 47 (March 1966): 201–203.

RIT Reporter 1966
"The School for American Craftsmen." *RIT Reporter* 41 (February 11, 1966).

RIT Reporter 1966a
"Film Wins Award; Produced by SAC." *RIT Reporter* 41 (May 27, 1966).

Romm 1966
Romm, Ethel G. "Fantasy Furniture." *Middletown [N.Y.] Times Herald Record* (March 7, 1966), 11.

Waldon 1966
Waldon, Mary. "Furniture in the Fantastic Style." *Indianapolis Star* (February 27, 1966), 5: 1.

1967

Cue 1967
"Exhibitions—Sculpted Furniture." *Cue* (April 20, 1967).

Esquire 1967
"October: Gifts Exclusive." *Esquire* 68 (October 1967): 154.

Giambruni 1967
Giambruni, Helen. "Exhibitions: Museum West." *Craft Horizons* 27 (March/April 1967): 46–47.

Moore 1967
Moore, Eudorah. "Exhibitions, California Capsule: Media Explored 1967." *Craft Horizons* 27 (May/June 1967): 56–58.

Whitaker 1967
Whitaker, Irwin. *Crafts and Craftsmen*. Dubuque, Iowa: William C. Brown, 1967 (p. 84).

1968

Crafts 1968
The Crafts and the Modern World. New York: Horizon Press, 1968.

Erdle 1968
Erdle, Penney. "It's a Work of Art as Well as a Desk." *Rochester Democrat and Chronicle* (October 13, 1968), B: 4.

Giambruni 1968
Giambruni, Helen. "Exhibitions: Wendell Castle." *Craft Horizons* 28 (May/June 1968): 54.

Giambruni 1968a
Giambruni, Helen. "Wendell Castle." *Craft Horizons* 28 (September/October 1968): 28–31, 50–51.

Interiors 1968
"News: Avant-Garde on Eighth Avenue." *Interiors* 77 (April 1968): 8.

Meilach 1968
Meilach, Dona Z. *Contemporary Art with Wood: Creative Techniques and Appreciation*. New York: Crown Publishers, 1968 (p. 185).

Newsweek 1968
"Life and Leisure: Furniture from Timber—Limber Timber." *Newsweek* 71 (May 13, 1968): 95.

Pahlman 1968
Pahlman, William. "A Matter of Taste: New Furniture Designed Like Massive Sculpture." *White Plains [N.Y.] Reporter Dispatch* (May 16, 1968).

Raven 1968
Raven, Theo and Peter. "Exhibitions: Letter from Seattle." *Craft Horizons* 28 (November/December 1968): 41–42.

Reif 1968
Reif, Rita. *Living with Books*. New York: New York Times Press, 1968 (pp. 116–117).

Reif 1968a
Reif, Rita. "Furniture That Seems to Be Growing." *New York Times* (April 9, 1968): 50.

Rochester Democrat and Chronicle 1968
"Sittin' Fancy." *Rochester Democrat and Chronicle* (June 24, 1968).

Rochester Democrat and Chronicle 1968a
"Nanci—Some Concepts of Art." *Rochester Democrat and Chronicle* (October 25, 1968), B: 6.

Rochester Democrat and Chronicle 1968b
"Nanci: Swinging, Singing in Everybody's Bag at Top of the Plaza." *Rochester Democrat and Chronicle* (November 4, 1968), B: 9.

Rochester Democrat and Chronicle 1968c
"Scottsville Craftsman Creates Usable Sculpture." *Rochester Democrat and Chronicle, Upstate Magazine* (November 17, 1968), cover, 22–27.

Simon 1968
Simon, Rita. "In the Galleries: Wendell Castle." *Arts Magazine* 42 (May 1968): 64.

Simpson 1968
Simpson, Thomas. *Fantasy Furniture: Design and Decoration*. New York: Reinhold Book Corp., 1968 (pp. 82, 90, 94).

Willcox 1968
Willcox, Donald. *Wood Design*. New York: Watson-Guptill, 1968 (pp. 66–67, 85–87).

1969

Bergmanis 1969
Bergmanis, Talis. "Old Clothes Return to Rochester." *Rochester Democrat and Chronicle, Upstate Magazine* (April 20, 1969), 4–5.

Breckenridge 1969
Breckenridge, Bruce. "Exhibitions: Wisconsin Designer-Craftsmen." *Craft Horizons* 29 (July/August 1969): 39–51.

Castle 1969
Castle, Wendell. "Mike Nevelson: The Gender of Wood." *Craft Horizons* 29 (March 1969): 16–21.

Castle 1969a
Castle, Wendell. "Finger Lakes Exhibitions." *Craft Horizons* 29 (September/October 1969): 67–68.

Castle 1969b
Castle, Wendell. "Penland Resident Craftsmen." *Craft Horizons* 29 (September/October 1969): 68.

Conroy 1969
Conroy, Sarah Booth. "American Contemporary Crafts: Too Individualistic for Label." *New York Times* (October 3, 1969), C: 48.

Emporia Gazette 1969
"Former Emporian Now Designing Imaginative Sculptured Furniture." *Emporia [Kans.] Gazette* (October 28, 1969).

Getlein 1969
Getlein, Frank. "New Things Are Happening in Same Old Media." *Washington Sunday Star* (October 5, 1969).

Gingrich 1969
Gingrich, Arnold. *Business and the Arts: An Answer to Tomorrow.* New York: Paul S. Eriksson, 1969 (p. 79).

Hoffman 1969
Hoffman, Donald. "A Room Is Peopled by Its Furniture?" *Kansas City [Mo.] Star* (July 20, 1969), D: 2.

Home Furnishings Daily 1969
"Objects: USA." *Home Furnishings Daily* (September 8, 1969).

Newsweek 1969
"Art: Crafting Their Own World." *Newsweek* 74 (July 21, 1969): 62–65.

Pearce 1969
Pearce, Dennis. "Furniture Is Sculptured." *Wichita Eagle* (May 28, 1969).

Scottsville News 1969
"Film to Be Shown on Local Sculptor." *Scottsville [N.Y.] News* (June 19, 1969).

Secrest 1969
Secrest, Meryle. "'Objects: USA'—More Art Than Crafts." *Washington Post* (October 3, 1969), C: 1, 8.

Simmons 1969
Simmons, Robert Hilton. "Objects: USA, the Johnson Collection of Contemporary Crafts." *Craft Horizons* 29 (November/December 1969): 24–51, 66.

Vicente 1969
Vicente, Harriet. "Exhibitions: The Excellence of the Object." *Craft Horizons* 29 (May/June 1969): 59–60.

1970

Architectural Forum 1970
"Forum: Environment—Tune-out, Turn-in, Take-off." *Architectural Forum* 132 (March 1970): 20.

Ashbery 1970
Ashbery, John. "The Johnson Collection at Cranbrook." *Craft Horizons* 30 (March/April 1970): 35, 57–58, 70.

Brighton-Pittsford Post 1970
"Wendell Castle Joins Brockport." *Brighton-Pittsford [N.Y.] Post* (July 23, 1970).

Castle 1970
Castle, Wendell. "Wharton Esherick 1887–1970." *Craft Horizons* 30 (August 1970): 10–17.

Craft Horizons 1970
"Our Contributors." *Craft Horizons* 30 (August 1970): 5.

El-Zoghby 1970
El-Zoghby, Gamal. "Designed for Contemplation." *Craft Horizons* 30 (March/April 1970): 12–19, 55.

Feldman 1970
Feldman, Edmund Burke. *Becoming Human through Art: Aesthetic Experience in the School.* Englewood Cliffs, N.J.: Prentice-Hall, 1970 (p. 249).

Feldman 1970a
Feldman, Edmund Burke. *Varieties of Visual Experience.* Englewood Cliffs, N.J.: Prentice-Hall, 1970 (p. 492).

Geft 1970
Geft, Olga. "Exhibition Notes." *Interiors* 129 (March 1970): 18.

Kay 1970
Kay, Jane Holtz. "Exhibitions: Crafts 1970." *Craft Horizons* 30 (May/June 1970): 54.

New York Magazine 1970
"Art: Some New Dodges, or Room to Ponder." *New York Magazine* (January 26, 1970): 58.

Nordness 1970
Nordness, Lee. *Objects USA.* New York: Viking Press, 1970 (pp. 243, 256–257).

Palo Alto Times 1970
"Furniture with a Sculptural Flourish." *Palo Alto [Calif.] Times* (December 11, 1970), 2: 11.

Plumb 1970
Plumb, Barbara. "The Space Shapers." *American Home* 73 (May 1970): 26–38.

Progressive Architecture 1970
"Museum Provides Exhibits for Contemplation." *Progressive Architecture* 51 (March 1970): 42.

Rogers 1970
Rogers, Susan. "Meditating on Fifty-third Street." *New York Post* (January 21, 1970).

Rogers 1970a
Rogers, Susan. "Lamps: From the Floor Up." *New York Post* (March 24, 1970), 50.

Teres 1970
Teres, Rosemary. "Exhibitions: Wendell Castle." *Craft Horizons* 30 (March/April 1970): 44.

Time 1970
"Art: Time for Space." *Time* 95 (February 2, 1970): 43–44.

Village Voice 1970
"Sixteen Environments." *Village Voice* (January 22, 1970), 47.

Virginia Museum Members Bulletin 1970
"The Crafts Juror." *Virginia Museum Members Bulletin* 30 (February 1970).

1971

Conroy 1971
Conroy, Sarah Booth. "Wood Craftsman Esherick: Holdout in an Age of Plastic." *Washington Post* (October 10, 1971), K: 1, 7.

Craft Horizons 1971
"Craftsmen's World: New Shops and Galleries Flourish Despite Economy." *Craft Horizons* 31 (December 1971): 5–6.

Creative Guidelines 1971
"Plastic Products." *Creative Guidelines: A Newsletter Serving the Furnishings Industry* 2 (April 17, 1971).

Lewis 1971
Lewis, Peggy. "Exhibitions: Contemporary Crafts." *Craft Horizons* 31 (March/April 1971): 50.

Peterson 1971
Peterson, Allan. "Exhibitions: Nancy Jurs—Wendell Castle." *Craft Horizons* 31 (December 1971): 54.

Reeves 1971
Reeves, Jean. "Bright, Plastic World for Furniture 'Collector.'" *Buffalo Evening News* (October 25, 1971), A: 6.

Reif 1971
Reif, Rita. "U.S. Furniture Designers Find a New Market for Their Talents." *New York Times* (April 24, 1971), C: 34.

Vogue 1971
"Fashions in Living: The Decorating Scoop." *Vogue* 158 (September 15, 1971): 30.

Willig 1971
Willig, Nancy. "Interesting Show at Gallery West." *Buffalo Courier-Express* (October 15, 1971), 28.

1972

Conroy 1972
Conroy, Sarah Booth. "Woodenworks: Elevating the Everyday." *Washington Post* (January 23, 1972), H: 1, 3.

Craft Horizons 1972
"The Craftsman's World: Renwick Gallery Opens as National Showcase for Craft and Design." *Craft Horizons* 32 (February 1972): 3.

Craft Horizons 1972a
"In Brief." *Craft Horizons* 32 (February 1972): 52.

Dienstag 1972
Dienstag, Eleanor. "Happy Birthday, Shop One." *Rochester Democrat and Chronicle, Upstate Magazine* (September 24, 1972), 18–22.

Emerson 1972
Emerson, Paul. "Sterling Associates Top in Field." *Palo Alto [Calif.] Times* (March 10, 1972), B: 9.

Giddins 1972
Giddins, Susan Rogers. "The Craft Show Comes to Town." *New York Post* (July 3, 1972), 24.

McFarland 1972
McFarland, Gay. "Stendig Takes Comfort with a Sense of Humor." *Houston Post* (November 26, 1972), AA: 10.

National Community Arts Program 1972
U.S. Department of Housing and Urban Development, Washington, D.C. *National Community Arts Program.* 1972 (p. 12).

Newman 1972
Newman, Thelma R. *Plastics as Design Forms.* Philadelphia: Chilton Press, 1972 (pp. 114, 290, 291).

Peterson 1972
Peterson, Allan. "Exhibitions: Radial 80." *Craft Horizons* 32 (April 1972): 51.

Rochester Democrat and Chronicle 1972
"Castle Exhibiting." *Rochester Democrat and Chronicle* (January 26, 1972), C: 1.

Rossbach 1972
Rossbach, Ed. "Objects: USA Revisited." *Craft Horizons* 32 (August 1972): 38–39.

Saiberlich 1972
Saiberlich, Bette. "Exhibitions: New York State Craftsmen—1972 Selections." *Craft Horizons* 32 (June 1972): 49.

Schorr 1972
Schorr, Mimi. "A Survey of Crafts Today." *American Artist* 36 (April 1972): 20–25, 78–80.

Sokolov 1972
Sokolov, Raymond A. "All in One Spot: Kitchenware from the Very Old to the Modern." *New York Times* (September 21, 1972), C: 56.

Watk 1972
Watk, Joan Pearson. "Pomp and Circumstance: The Renwick Gallery Opens for the Exhibition of Arts, Crafts, and Design in the Grand Manner." *Craft Horizons* 32 (April 1972): 44–45, 68–70.

1973

Bowden 1973
Bowden, Craig, Nancy, and Mary. "Holiday Gifting: Gifts You Couldn't Give Before." *House Beautiful* 115 (December 1973): 58–65.

Craft Horizons 1973
"Craft News: Commissions and Acquisitions." *Craft Horizons* 32 (April 1973): 6.

Eisenberg 1973
Eisenberg, D. D. "You Fill the Cavity in This Big, Plastic Tooth." *Philadelphia Evening Bulletin* (August 2, 1973), B: 28.

Ogden 1973
Ogden, Anne. "Designing Their Own Lifestyle: Two Craftsmen Forge an Environment That Brings Home and Work Together." *House Beautiful* 115 (June 1973): 70–74.

Wendell Castle Associates 1973
Wendell Castle Associates, Rochester, New York. *The Molar Group.* Brochure. May 1973.

1974

Dardenne 1974
Dardenne, Bob. "The Swirling City." *Rochester Times-Union* (May 23, 1974), C: 1–2.

Donohoe 1974
Donohoe, Victoria. "At the Museum: A Fine Mixed Bag." *Philadelphia Inquirer* (February 24, 1974), K: 9.

Newman 1974
Newman, Thelma R. *Plastics as Sculpture.* Philadelphia: Chilton Press, 1974 (pp. 113–114).

Rhodes 1974
Rhodes, Lynette. "Exhibitions: Nine Artisans." *Craft Horizons* 34 (April 1974): 50.

Teres 1974
Teres, Rosemary. "'Provincial' Artists and Craftsmen Steal the Show in 'Radial 80' at Xerox Square." *Rochester Times-Union* (February 23, 1974), C: 3.

Walsh 1974
Walsh, Sally. "Most See 'The Twist' as Symbol of Hope for Downtown Area." *Rochester Democrat and Chronicle* (June 4, 1974), C: 1.

Walsh 1974a
Walsh, Sally. "Rochester's Shop One—One of the Best?" *Rochester Democrat and Chronicle* (December 19, 1974), C: 1–2.

Wild 1974
Wild, Patricia L. "As Readers See It—'Sculpture in Park a Welcome Addition.'" *Rochester Times-Union* (June 15, 1974), A: 6.

1975

City/East 1975
"Gannett's Staying Downtown—In a Crafty Style." *City/East* (Rochester) 6 (October 21, 1975).

Craft Horizons 1975
"Craft Multiples." *Craft Horizons* 35 (August 1975): 32–35.

Crowther 1975
Crowther, Hal. "Burchfield Center: Exhibit of Woodcraft Carves Niche in Art." *Buffalo Evening News* (October 21, 1975).

Cullinan 1975
Cullinan, Helen. "Sculptors Get Their Day to Show." *Cleveland Plain Dealer* (October 26, 1975): 11.

Hill 1975
Hill, June. "Fun for Furnishings." *Chicago Tribune* (May 25, 1975), C: 1, 10.

Meilach 1975
Meilach, Dona Z. *Creating Modern Furniture: Trends, Techniques, Appreciation.* New York: Crown Publishers, 1975 (pp. 23, 28, 137, 150, 167, 287).

Meyer 1975
Meyer, Carolyn. *People Who Make Things: How American Craftsmen Live and Work.* New York: Atheneum, 1975 (pp. 166–173).

Miller 1975
Miller, Jamie. "The Castles' Castle." *Rochester Democrat and Chronicle, Upstate Magazine* (May 25, 1975): 12–17.

Skurka 1975
Skurka, Norma. "Design: Baronial, Updated." *New York Times Magazine* (August 3, 1975), 34.

Walsh 1975
Walsh, Sally. "Art—On Modern Sculpture and the Taxpayers' Money." *Rochester Democrat and Chronicle* (December 14, 1975), G: 1, 4.

Willig 1975
Willig, Nancy Tobin. "Burchfield Center Review: Language of Wood Defined." *Buffalo Courier-Express* (October 24, 1975).

1976

Castle 1976
Castle, Wendell. "Design Considerations: Thoughts on Form, Materials, and Techniques." *Fine Woodworking* 1 (Winter 1976): 27.

Donohoe 1976
Donohoe, Victoria. "Handmade Furniture Shows Individualism." *Philadelphia Inquirer* (February 6, 1976), D: 3.

Hammel 1976
Hammel, Lisa. "Two Designers Have a Way with Wood." *New York Times* (August 19, 1976), 40.

Kelsey 1976
Kelsey, John. "Stacking: The Technique of Building up Wood Forms for Carving." *Fine Woodworking* 1 (Winter 1976): 22–26.

Kelsey 1976a
Kelsey, John. "The Woodcraft Scene: Craftsman's Gallery." *Fine Woodworking* 1 (Summer 1976): 10.

Makepeace 1976
Makepeace, John. "Wood-Working, an Appraisal by John Makepeace." In *Decorative Art and Modern Interiors 1975/76*, vol. 65, edited by Maria Scholfield. New York: Viking Press, 1976.

News from the Fendrick Gallery 1976
"In October." *News from the Fendrick Gallery* (September 1976).

Rochester Democrat and Chronicle 1976
"Bean Barn Art." *Rochester Democrat and Chronicle, Upstate Magazine* (May 9, 1976), 39.

Shutt 1976
Shutt, Carol. "Exhibitions: Hardwood Furniture and Objects: Winter 1976." *Craft Horizons* 35 (August 1976): 61.

1977

Becker 1977
Becker, Missy. "The Artist-Craftsman." *Town and Country* (October 1977): 178–179.

Belvin 1977
Belvin, Marjorie Elliott. *Design through Discovery.* New York: Holt, Rinehart, and Winston, 1977.

Carr 1977
Carr, Genie. "Sculpted Furniture." *Winston-Salem [N.C.] Sentinel* (April 27, 1977), 13, 20.

Conroy 1977
Conroy, Sarah Booth. "Great Gourmet! Artful Attitudes on America's Table." *Washington Post* (March 27, 1977), G: 1, 3.

Conroy 1977a
Conroy, Sarah Booth. "GSA's Master Builder: Images and Ideals." *Washington Post* (October 28, 1977), L: 1–2.

Donohoe 1977
Donohoe, Victoria. "A Richness in Woodworking." *Philadelphia Inquirer* (August 19, 1977), 23.

Donohoe 1977a
Donohoe, Victoria. "The Work of the Woodcrafter: Nostalgic Look at Americana." *Philadelphia Inquirer* (December 23, 1977), 29.

Euaclaire 1977
Euaclaire, Sally. "'Artmaker' Castle: Revolution in Furniture." *Rochester Democrat and Chronicle* (September 18, 1977), E: 1, 6.

Hall 1977
Hall, Julie. *Tradition and Change: The New American Craftsmen.* New York: E. P. Dutton, 1977 (pp. 52, 54, 59).

Hammel 1977
Hammel, Lisa. "For American Craftsmen, a Coming of Age." *New York Times* (June 16, 1977), C: 8.

Holton Recorder 1977
"Award for Staircase." *Holton [Kans.] Recorder* 109 (December 19, 1977).

Rochester Democrat and Chronicle 1977
"Art: Fairchild Award to Castle." *Rochester Democrat and Chronicle* (November 19, 1977), C: 1.

Williams 1977
Williams, Jeannie. "Gannett's New Corporate Home." *Rochester Times-Union* (January 10, 1977), C: 1, 4–5.

Williams 1977a
Williams, Jeannie. "Breezy Weekend: 39,000 Hang Out at Clothesline." *Rochester Times-Union* (September 12, 1977), C: 1, 5.

Williams 1977b
Williams, Jeannie. "You Can 'Vote' on 'Artmakers' Sunday." *Rochester Times-Union* (September 23, 1977), C: 1.

1978

Conroy 1978
Conroy, Sarah Booth. "Vladimir Kagan's Soft Touch." *International Herald Tribune* (September 1, 1978), 14.

Euaclaire 1978
Euaclaire, Sally. "Fooling the Eye in Carved Wood." *Rochester Democrat and Chronicle* (October 8, 1978), E: 1, 4.

Euaclaire 1978a
Euaclaire, Sally. "Wendell Castle: Wood, Form, and Space." *Craft Horizons* 38 (December 1978): 60–65.

Edgar 1978
Edgar, Natalie. "Sixteen American Woodcarvers." *Craft Horizons* 38 (April 1978): 36–37.

Foran 1978
Foran, Jack. "Art: NCCC's 'Fantasy '78' Artists Let Loose." *Niagara [N.Y.] Gazette* (March 19, 1978).

Herzig 1978
Herzig, Doris. "Twentieth-Century Quality." *New York Newsday* (February 25, 1978), part 2, A: 2–3.

Herzig 1978a
Herzig, Doris. "A Furniture Maker's Artistic Twist." *New York Newsday* (May 20, 1978), part 2, A: 2–3.

Kelsey 1978
Kelsey, John. *Stacking: The Technique of Building-up Wood Forms for Carving.* Fine Woodworking Techniques 1: Selected by the Editors of *Fine Woodworking* Magazine. Newtown, Conn.: Taunton Press, 1978.

Niagara Gazette 1978
"'Fantasy' Shown." *Niagara [N.Y.] Gazette* (February 23, 1978), 2.

Norklun 1978
Norklun, Kathi. "Wendell Castle, 'Furniture as Art,' at Fendrick Gallery." *Washington Review* (October 1978): 21–22.

Page 1978
Page, Sharon. "Furniture as an Art Form, Twenty-eight Pieces of Wendell Castle's Handcrafted, Sculptural Furniture Get Artistic Status at the Fendrick." *Washington Star* (October 15, 1978), 20–21.

Platt 1978
Platt, John. *Step-by-Step Woodcraft: A Complete Introduction to the Craft of Woodworking*. New York: Golden Press, 1978 (pp. 15, 50).

Reif 1978
Reif, Rita. "A Show at the Met on What's Out of Fashion." *New York Times* (March 2, 1978), M: 23.

Russell 1978
Russell, John. "Gallery View: The Met Salutes the Decorative." *New York Times* (February 19, 1978), 29, 32.

Stanley 1978
Stanley, Marsha. "Limited Edition Art Furniture: One Way to Lower the Cost of Wendell Castle Pieces Is to Mass Produce Them. Well, Sort of. . . ." *Rochester Democrat and Chronicle, Upstate Magazine* (March 26, 1978): 28–31.

Washingtonian 1978
"Form Follows Function?" *Washingtonian* (February 1978): 27.

1979

American Craft 1979
"Working Wonders with Wood: American Furniture Makers Working in Hardwood." *American Craft* 39 (June/July 1979): 10–15.

American Craft 1979/80
"Exhibitions: Wendell Castle—Albert Paley—Frans Wildenhain." *American Craft* 39 (December 1979/ January 1980): 59–60.

Castle 1979
Castle, Wendell. "Parnham House: School for Craftsmen in Wood." *Craft Horizons* 39 (April 1979): 49.

Chapple and Watterland 1979
Chapple, Abby, and Michael Watterland. "Arts and Crafts: VP Style." *Washington Star* (September 30, 1979), 20.

Craft Horizons 1979
"Museum Reopens with Handmade Furniture." *Craft Horizons* 39 (April 1979): 43.

Feldkamp 1979
Feldkamp, Phyllis. "Craftsmen Warm Up to Wood." *Philadelphia Bulletin* (July 3, 1979), A: 27.

Hunter-Stiebel 1979/80
Hunter-Stiebel, Penelope. [Reinstallation of modern decorative arts galleries.] *Metropolitan Museum of Art Bulletin* 37 (Winter 1979/80): 50–51.

Lucie-Smith 1979
Lucie-Smith, Edward. *Furniture: A Concise History*. London: Oxford University Press, 1979 (p. 206).

Polmenteer 1979
Polmenteer, Vaughn. "Crafted by Castle; the Church Is Neo-Gothic, but the Renovated Chancel Is Strictly Wendell Castle." *Rochester Democrat and Chronicle, Upstate Magazine* (September 23, 1979), cover, 4–12.

Rochester Times-Union 1979
"Tip Off on the Arts: It's Dr. Castle." *Rochester Times-Union* (May 25, 1979), C: 3.

Rochester Times-Union 1979a
"Tip Off on the Arts: Umbrellas for the Mondales." *Rochester Times-Union* (November 2, 1979), C: 3.

Stapleton 1979/80
Stapleton, Constance. "Crafts in the Vice-Presidential Collection." *American Craft* 39 (December 1979/January 1980): 24–27.

Williams 1979
Williams, Jeannie. "Two for the Shows." *Rochester Times-Union* (October 15, 1979), C: 1, 4.

1980

American Craft 1980/81
"Exhibitions: Wendell Castle." *American Craft* 40 (December 1980/January 1981): 68.

Bennett 1980
Bennett, Judy. "Design for Celebrities." *Rochester Democrat and Chronicle* (November 2, 1980), D: 1, 6.

Brighton-Pittsford Post 1980
"Wendell Castle Exhibits in D.C." *Brighton-Pittsford [N.Y.] Post* (November 6, 1980), B: 13.

Castle and Edman 1980
Castle, Wendell, and David Edman. *The Wendell Castle Book of Wood Lamination*. New York: Van Nostrand Reinhold Co., 1980.

Conroy 1980
Conroy, Sarah Booth. "The Art You Would Love to Use." *Washington Post* (November 16, 1980), K: 3.

Garner 1980
Garner, Philippe. *The Contemporary Decorative Arts from 1940 to the Present Day*. New York: Phaidon Press, 1980 (pp. 24, 79, 206–207).

Garner 1980a
Garner, Philippe. *Twentieth-Century Furniture*. New York: Van Nostrand Reinhold Co., 1980 (pp. 206–207).

Interior Design 1980
"Interior Design Market: Wendell Castle." *Interior Design* 51 (April 1980): 186.

Interior Design 1980a
"The Wendell Castle Workshop." *Interior Design* 51 (July 1980): 37.

Kohen 1980
Kohen, Helen L. "Funny Forms Mask Fine Designs." *Miami Herald* (June 13, 1980), D: 7.

Lewis 1980
Lewis, Jo Ann. "Unusual Gifts from Bugs to Blocks." *Washington Post* (December 13, 1980), D: 7.

Lucie-Smith 1980
Lucie-Smith, Edward. *Art in the Seventies*. New York: Phaidon Press, 1980 (pp. 58–59, 122–123).

Rochester City Newspaper 1980
"Art in Rochester." *Rochester City Newspaper* (September 25, 1980), A: 1–3.

Roukes 1980
Roukes, Nicholas. *Masters of Wood Sculpture*. New York: Watson-Guptill, 1980 (p. 147).

Washington Star 1980
"An Exhibition of Furniture by Wendell Castle." *Washington Star* (November 21, 1980).

1981

Dudgeon 1981
Dudgeon, Piers. *The Art of Making Furniture*. New York: Sterling Publishing Co., 1981.

Fairbanks and Bates 1981
Fairbanks, Jonathan L., and Elizabeth Bidwell Bates. *American Furniture 1620 to the Present*. New York: Richard Marek Publishers, 1981 (pp. 521–522, 526).

Fine Woodworking 1981
"Royal Suite." *Fine Woodworking* 31 (November/ December 1981): back cover.

Heckscher 1981
Heckscher, August. "American Craft Museum: Twenty-five Years." *American Craft* 41 (October/ November 1981): 9–17.

Ohio Arts Council 1981
"Furniture as Sculpture: Handcrafted Wood Furniture by Five Contemporary Artists." *Ohio Arts Council, Dialogue* (May/June 1981): 23.

Peters 1981
Peters, Susan Dodge. "Furniture as Art." *Rochester City Newspaper* (November 25, 1981), 13.

Portland Oregonian 1981
"Twenty-seven Artists Remain in Running for Justice Center Works." *Portland Oregonian* (May 1, 1981), F: 4.

Prichard 1981
Prichard, Ann. "Furniture as Fine Art." *Rochester Times-Union* (November 5, 1981), C: 1, 2.

Rochester Democrat and Chronicle 1981
"Fine Art of Furniture Making." *Rochester Democrat and Chronicle* (November 1, 1981), D: 1.

Rochester Democrat and Chronicle 1981a
"Magazine Features Junior League Showhouse Display." *Rochester Democrat and Chronicle* (November 8, 1981), D: 4.

Rochester Times-Union 1981
"Tip Off on the Arts: Nice Words for Wendell." *Rochester Times-Union* (January 16, 1981), C: 3.

Russell 1981
Russell, John. "Wendell Castle and Arlene Slavin." *New York Times* (January 9, 1981), C: 19.

Seltzer 1981
Seltzer, Ruth. "Joan Mondale Busy at the Museum." *Philadelphia Inquirer* (June 9, 1981), D: 2.

Sporkin 1981
Sporkin, Elizabeth. "Modern Masters of Wood." *Washington Post* (March 1, 1981).

Stewart 1981
Stewart, Laura. "In Review/Art: More than Just Fine Furniture." *Rochester Democrat and Chronicle* (November 9, 1981), C: 1, 3.

Village Voice 1981
"Art: Wendell Castle." *Village Voice* (January 7–13, 1981), 52.

G. Williams 1981
Williams, Gerry, ed. *Apprenticeship in Craft.* Goffstown, N.H.: Daniel Clark Books, 1981 (pp. 130–131).

J. Williams 1981
Williams, Jeannie. "A Little Friendly Bidding." *Rochester Times-Union* (October 28, 1981), C: 1–2.

Yoskowitz 1981
Yoskowitz, Robert. "Wendell Castle/Arlene Slavin." *Arts Magazine* 55 (March 1981): 25.

1982

Abercrombie 1982
Abercrombie, Stanley. "Furnishings: The Changing Wonders of Wendell Castle." *AIA Journal* 71 (September 1982): 76–79.

Harrison 1982
Harrison, Helen. "Crafts and Art: Do They Differ?" *New York Times* (October 11, 1982), 1, 31.

Ketchum 1982
Ketchum, William C., Jr. *Chests, Cupboards, Desks, and Other Pieces.* New York: Alfred A. Knopf, 1982 (no. 321).

Osso 1982
Osso, M. C. "The Season: Art and Artists—Handcrafted Masterpieces." *Hamptons [N.Y.] Newspaper/Magazine* (May 27, 1982), 4.

Pritam and Eames 1982
Pritam and Eames Gallery, East Hampton, New York. *Pritam and Eames Portfolio.* 1982.

SLAM *Annual Report* 1982
St. Louis Art Museum. *Annual Report* (1982).

Von Eckhardt 1982
Von Eckhardt, Wolf. "Giving a Second Life to Trees: The Popularity of Handcrafted Wood Furniture Is Booming." *Time* 119 (June 21, 1982): 63–65.

Who's Who 1982–83
"Castle, Wendell." *Who's Who in America, 1982–1983.* Chicago: Marquis, 1982.

1983

Andrews 1983
Andrews, Chris. "Wendell Castle." *Art/World: Latest Museum Gallery Guide* 7 (April 1983): 4, 12.

Art: Das Kunstmagazin 1983
"Personalien." *Art: Das Kunstmagazin* 6 (June 1983).

Art Now 1983
"New York: Wendell Castle at Alexander F. Milliken." *Art Now/USA: The National Art Museum and Gallery Guide* 2 (March/April 1983): cover, N.Y. sect., 12.

ASID Newsletter 1983
"American Living National Treasures." *American Society of Interior Designers/Potomac Chapter Newsletter* 3 (May/June 1983): 1.

Bertorelli 1983
Bertorelli, Paul. "Two Schools: Castle and Krenov—Different Ideas about How to Teach." *Fine Woodworking* 39 (March/April 1983): 103–104.

Bethany 1983
Bethany, Marilyn. "Interior Trends 1984." *New York Times Magazine* (August 28, 1983): 52.

Brayer 1983
Brayer, Betsy. "New Direction in Furniture by Wendell Castle." *Brighton-Pittsford [N.Y.] Post* (April 13, 1983), B: 1–2.

Carpenter 1983
Carpenter, Arthur Espenet. "The Rise of Artiture: Woodworking Comes of Age." *Fine Woodworking* 38 (January/February 1983): 98–103.

Castle 1983
Castle, Wendell. "Neocon." *The Workshop: A Publication of the Wendell Castle Workshop* (Summer 1983): 13.

Chapman 1983
Chapman, Urbane [Anthony Urbane Chastain-Chapman]. "Wendell Castle Tries Elegance . . . and Pushes the Limits of Craftsmanship." *Fine Woodworking* 42 (September/October 1983): 68–73.

Contract 1983
"The World of Executive Desks." *Contract: The Business Magazine of Commercial Furnishings and Interior Architecture* 25 (September 1983): 152.

Davies 1983
Davies, Karen. "American Decorative Arts of the Late 1920s." *Antiques* 124 (December 1983): 1212–1217.

Daw 1983
Daw, Deborah. "Arts and Crafts." *Portfolio* 5 (July/August 1983): 58–63.

Degener 1983
Degener, Patricia. "Woodworkers Carve Out Modern Classics." *St. Louis Post Dispatch* (September 9, 1983), D: 1.

Della Corte 1983
Della Corte, Evelyn. "Product Extra: Ornamentalism." *Interiors* 142 (March 1983): cover, 130–131.

Diamonstein 1983
Diamonstein, Barbaralee. *Handmade in America.* New York: Harry N. Abrams, 1983 (pp. 25–37).

Epstein 1983
Epstein, Jason. "The Dealer's Eye—The Fine Line from Pritam and Eames: An Unassuming East Hampton Shop Deals in One-of-a-Kind Handcrafted Furniture." *House and Garden* 155 (August 1983): 24–26.

Giovannini 1983
Giovannini, Joseph. "Furniture for the Post-Modern Interior." *New York Times* (August 18, 1983), C: 1, 8.

Gunlocke 1983
Gunlocke Company, Wayland, New York. *Utopian Collection.* Brochure. 1983.

Interior Design 1983
"Interior Design Market: Wendell Castle for Gunlocke." *Interior Design* 54 (October 1983): 150.

Interiors 1983
"Designers Saturday: A New Graphic Dimension for Furniture Design." *Interiors* 143 (September 1983): 123–129.

Jensen and Conway 1983
Jensen, Robert, and Patricia Conway. *Ornamentalism: The New Decorativeness in Architecture and Design.* New York: Clarkson N. Potter, 1983 (pp. 216–223).

Kamm 1983
Kamm, Dorothy. "Castle's Fantasy Furniture." *Nit & Wit, Chicago's Art Magazine* (May/June 1983): 24–25.

Kelsey 1983
Kelsey, John. "Notes and Comments/Much Talk about Perfect Craftsmanship." *Fine Woodworking* 42 (September/October 1983): 98.

Lewis 1983
Lewis, Jo Ann. "Arts/Galleries: Decorative Crafts as Art." *Washington Post* (May 19, 1983).

Lichtenstein 1983
Lichtenstein, Therese. "Reviews: Wendell Castle." *Arts Magazine* 57 (May 1983): 49–50.

Lovenheim 1983
Lovenheim, Barbara. "Craftsman Carves a Niche for Himself." *Wall Street Journal* (December 19, 1983), 22.

Pearson 1983
Pearson, Katherine. *American Crafts: A Sourcebook for the Home.* New York: Stewart, Tabori and Chang, 1983 (pp. 99, 105, fig. 40).

Plakins 1983
Plakins, Ava. "Beast or Beauty?" *Connoisseur* 213 (February 1983): 18–19.

Plumb 1983
Plumb, Barbara. "Living—Precision." *Vogue* 173 (December 1983): 247.

Robins 1983
Robins, Marjorie K. "The Desk as a Thing of Beauty." *New York Newsday* (September 6, 1983), At Home section: 8, 9.

Russell 1983
Russell, John. "Wendell Castle." *New York Times* (March 18, 1983), C: 22.

Shopsin 1983
Shopsin, William C. "Opinion: Furniture As Art." *East Hampton [N.Y.] Star* (July 21, 1983), 11.

Slesin 1983
Slesin, Suzanne. "Technology and Tradition Mark Chicago Show." *New York Times* (June 16, 1983), C: 1, 6.

Stocker 1983
Stocker, Carol. "Classic Rock: An American Movement." *Boston Globe* (February 25, 1983): 25.

Story 1983
Story, Richard David. "Hot Properties." *Metropolitan Home* 15 (May 1983): 14–20.

1984

American Craft 1984
"Solid Color." *American Craft* 44 (June/July 1984): 28–31.

Caraldo 1984
Caraldo, Robert. "Galleries: Exploding the Borders." *New York Native* (May 21–June 3, 1984): 47–48.

Corporate Design 1984
"Corporate Art: Handcrafted Furniture for High-Tech Offices." *Corporate Design* 3 (September/October 1984): 89–90.

DiNoto 1984
DiNoto, Andrea. *Art Plastic: Designed for Living.* New York: Abbeville Press, 1984 (pp. 270–271).

Domergue 1984
Domergue, Denise. *Artists Design Furniture.* New York: Harry N. Abrams, 1984 (pp. 61–62).

Goldman 1984
Goldman, Elizabeth. "Material Evidence." *The Workshop: A Publication of the Wendell Castle Workshop* (Spring 1984): 1–3.

Hammel 1984
Hammel, Lisa. "The Expanding World of American Crafts." *New York Times* (June 28, 1984), C: 1, 6.

Hemphill 1984
Hemphill, Christopher. "Against the Grain: The Art of Wendell Castle." *Town and Country* (May 1984): 243–252.

Home Furnishings Daily 1984
"Furniture: Workbench Gallery Artisans Exhibit Designs in Colorcore." *Home Furnishings Daily* (April 16, 1984): 35.

Netsky 1984
Netsky, Ron. "Carving Out a Niche: RIT Adds Two Craftsmen to Staff, Putting School at Forefront of Fine Arts." *Rochester Democrat and Chronicle* (September 7, 1984), C: 1.

Progressive Architecture 1984
"P/A News Report—Colorcore II: The Master Craftsmen." *Progressive Architecture* 65 (May 1984): 21.

Rochester Times-Union 1984
"Craftsmen of Renown to Play Dual Role on the RIT Faculty." *Rochester Times-Union* (September 6, 1984), C: 1.

Roszkiewicz 1984
Roszkiewicz, Ron. *The Woodturner's Companion.* New York: Sterling Publishing Co., 1984 (p. 43).

Russell 1984
Russell, John. "Furniture Reveals the Artist's Touch." *New York Times* (July 5, 1984), C: 1, 9.

Slesin 1984
Slesin, Suzanne. "Home Beat: Taking a New Tack." *New York Times* (April 19, 1984), C: 3.

Szenasy 1984
Szenasy, Susan S. *Office Furniture.* New York: Facts on File, 1984 (pp. 83, 93).

1985

Adler 1985
Adler, Jane. "Furnishings That Fit Human Shape May Find Home away from Office." *Providence Sunday Journal* (October 6, 1985), F: 6.

Beale and Hedgecock 1985
Beale, Lewis, and Cathy Hedgecock. "Making It in Crafts." *Venture* (May 1985): 64–72.

Boyce 1985
Boyce, Charles. *Dictionary of Furniture.* New York: Roundtable Press, 1985 (p. 50).

Brown 1985
Brown, Patricia Leigh. "Castle: A Craftsman Considered a King." *Philadelphia Inquirer* (December 15, 1985), K: 1, 11.

Brown 1985a
Brown, Patricia Leigh. "Artful Touch Redefines Furniture." *Orlando [Fla.] Sentinel* (December 29, 1985), D: 1, 8.

Carlson 1985
Carlson, Lavonne. "Function, Traditions Stressed in Laguna Art Exhibit." *Austin Daily Texan* (June 5, 1985), 13.

Changing Times 1985
"To Get the Best, Have It Made: Custom-Made Furniture Is as Unique as You Are." *Changing Times* (April 1985): 75.

Cincinnati Downtowner 1985
"Contemporary Furniture on Exhibit at Taft Museum." *Cincinnati Downtowner* (September 9–15, 1985), 2.

Connoisseur 1985
"Connoisseur's World: There Are Clocks and Then There Are Wendell Castle's Clocks." *Connoisseur* 215 (November 1985): 62.

Dimich 1985
Dimich, Carol D. "Datebook: Furniture Full of Surprises." *Washington Home*, supplement to the *Washington Post* (August 1, 1985): 24.

Dorsey 1985
Dorsey, John. "It's Furniture . . . and Sculpture." *Baltimore Sun* (August 4, 1985), F: 1, 10.

Findsen 1985
Findsen, Owen. "Furniture or Art? Furniture Again Is Being Appreciated as High Art Form." *Cincinnati Inquirer* (September 11, 1985), G: 1.

Findsen 1985a
Findsen, Owen. "Notice to Everyone Who Scoffed at Practical Art." *Cincinnati Inquirer* (September 29, 1985), G: 7.

Gimelson 1985
Gimelson, Deborah. "Art or Crafts?" *Art at Auction* 8 (October 1985): 102–104.

Hammel 1985
Hammel, Lisa. "The Highly Skilled Teamwork behind the Master Craftsman." *New York Times* (August 29, 1985), C: 1, 6.

Hammel 1985a
Hammel, Lisa. "A Woodworker's Show of Clocks." *New York Times* (November 14, 1985), C: 3.

Hehman 1985
Hehman, Maureen C. "Tipsheet: Furniture as Art." *Cincinnati Post* (September 10, 1985), B: 4.

Heller 1985
Heller, Linda. "A Guide to Manhattan's Galleries." *Diversion* (May 1985).

Hoffman 1985
Hoffman, Marilyn. "American Design 1900–1985: The Whitney Museum Exhibition of 20th-Century Design Highlights an Array of Modernist Trends." *Christian Science Monitor* (October 18, 1985): 29.

House Beautiful 1985
"HB Lookout—Events: Fathering Time." *House Beautiful* 127 (November 1985): 19.

Interior Design 1985
"Interior Design Market: Wendell Castle Designs for Father Time." *Interior Design* 56 (September 1985): 107.

Jacobson 1985
Jacobson, Sebby Wilson. "Keeping Ahead of His Time." *Rochester Times-Union* (November 26, 1985), C: 1, 5.

Jepson 1985
Jepson, Barbara. "Art Furniture . . . Conceived by a New Breed of Designer—Typically a Sculptor, Painter, Architect, or Craftsman by Background." *American Craft* 45 (October/November 1985): 10–17.

Kaufman 1985
Kaufman, Charles. "Artists Craft Materials into Innovative Works." *Austin [Tex.] American Statesman* (May 31, 1985), G: 1.

Kessler 1985
Kessler, Pamela. "Castle's Clocks That Strike the Eye." *Washington Post* (December 27, 1985).

Lewis 1985
Lewis, Jo Ann. "Galleries: Furniture at Fendrick Gallery." *Washington Post* (July 6, 1985), C: 7.

Lovenheim 1985
Lovenheim, Barbara. "Furniture Craftsmen." *America Illustrated* (September 1985), Russian edition.

Lucie-Smith 1985
Lucie-Smith, Edward. *American Art Now*. New York: William Morrow and Co., 1985 (pp. 7–71).

McCombie 1985
McCombie, Mel. "Review: Intimately Imaginative—Artists Create with Traditional Materials." *Austin [Tex.] American Statesman* (June 21, 1985), F: 1.

Netsky 1985
Netsky, Ron. "Fine Faculty Patchwork: Paley, Castle Works Provide a Firm Anchor for Exhibition at RIT." *Rochester Democrat and Chronicle* (January 27, 1985), D: 3.

RIT 1985
Rochester Institute of Technology, College of Fine and Applied Arts, Rochester, New York. *At RIT, Artists in the Renaissance of the Decorative Arts, Wendell Castle, Albert Paley*. Brochure. 1985.

Robinson 1985
Robinson, Rosemary. "Master Worker Wendell Castle's Long-Case Clocks Will Grace Two Major Exhibitions." *Brighton-Pittsford [N.Y.] Post* (November 21, 1985), B: 1–2.

Rogers 1985
Rogers, Patricia Dane. "Design: Handmade Furniture Rich with Allusion." *Washington Post* (April 25, 1985), 10, 12, 14.

St. Louis Post Dispatch 1985
"Extraordinary Wood, Extraordinary Craftsmen." *St. Louis Post Dispatch* (June 9, 1985).

Schaire 1985
Schaire, Jeffrey. "Wendell Castle's Clocks: The New Work of a Virtuoso Craftsman Poses Some Difficult Problems." *Art and Antiques* (October 1985): 67–69.

Shukalo 1985
Shukalo, Alice. "Painstaking Technique Defines Painter's Renaissance Touch." *Austin [Tex.] American Statesman* (June 13, 1985), D: 3.

Truppin 1985
Truppin, Andrea. "Special Report: Creative Editions—Windigo Architects Design a New Gallery for the Arc International Collection." *Interiors* 144 (May 1985): 294–297.

Warner 1985
Warner, Patricia. "Art Camouflaged as Furniture." *Studio International* 198, no. 1009 (1985): 10–14.

Welzenbach 1985
Welzenbach, Michael. "Fine Art of Furniture Displayed at Fendrick." *Washington Times* (August 29, 1985), B: 3.

1986

Allen 1986
Allen, Jane Addams. "Top Picks: Art." *Washington Times Magazine* (January 10, 1986), M: 18.

Ambiente 1986
"Notizen: Auf der Suche nach der Komischer Zeit." *Ambiente* (Offenburg, West Germany) 14 (March 1986): 22.

American Craft 1986
"Gallery: Wood—Wendell Castle." *American Craft* 46 (October/November 1986): 83.

Antiques and Arts Weekly 1986
"Masterpieces of Time: Clocks by Wendell Castle on View at Smithsonian's Renwick Gallery." *Antiques and Arts Weekly* (January 24, 1986), 52.

Art and Antiques 1986
"Marble and Mosaics." *Art and Antiques* (Summer 1986): 31.

Berman 1986
Berman, Avis. "The Craft of Art: Alexander and Bettina Milliken's SoHo Loft." *Architectural Digest* 43 (October 1986): 198–203.

Bond 1986
Bond, Constance. "Smithsonian Highlights: Wendell Castle's Intriguing Clocks." *Smithsonian Magazine* 16 (March 1986): 186.

Brighton-Pittsford Post 1986
"First Exclusive Exhibit of Castle School Faculty."
Brighton-Pittsford [N.Y.] Post (January 15, 1986),
B: 10.

Brown 1986
Brown, Patricia Leigh. "Castle Craft: Designer's
Furniture Builds Bridges into the Realm of Art."
Chicago Tribune (January 12, 1986), 15: 2.

Busch 1986
Busch, Akiko. "By Design: Timepieces for Thought."
Metropolis 5 (March 1986): 39–44.

Byers and Rosenfeld 1986
Byers, Margery, and Alvin Rosenfeld. "Not Just
Another Pretty Face." *Exhibit Magazine* (March/April
1986): 2–3.

Canty 1986
Canty, Donald. "Castle Turns to Towering Clocks."
Architecture 75 (February 1986): 22–23.

Castle 1986
Castle, Wendell. "The Leading Edge: What's
Happening with the Best Contemporary American
Furniture and Where It Came From." *Popular
Mechanics* 163 (November 1986): 86–90.

Chastain-Chapman 1986
Chastain-Chapman, Anthony Urbane. "Fine Time:
Wendell Castle's Baker's Dozen." *American Craft* 46
(April/May 1986): 18–25.

Conroy 1986
Conroy, Sarah Booth. "Art around the Clock."
Washington Post (January 1, 1986).

Dimich and Wexler 1986
Dimich, Carol, and Henrietta Wexler. "Decorative
Arts in Washington—Time and Defiance of Gravity,
Recent Works by Wendell Castle at the Renwick
Gallery." *Museum Washington* (September/October
1986): 50–52.

Donohoe 1986
Donohoe, Victoria. "A Balancing of Two Soloists and
a Group." *Philadelphia Inquirer* (December 12,
1986), 46.

Faulkner, Faulkner, and Nissen 1986
Faulkner, Roy, Sarah Faulkner, and LuAnn Nissen.
Inside Today's Home. New York: Holt, Rinehart,
and Winston, 1986 (pp. 163, 250, fig. 163).

Forsman 1986
Forsman, Theresa. "Furniture for Art's Sake."
Hackensack [N.J.] Record (July 6, 1986), F: 3.

Freedman 1986
Freedman, A. "Plastic Fantasies Made by Castle
the Wood Wizard." *Toronto Globe and Mail*
(October 4, 1986).

Ghent 1986
Ghent, Janet. "Aluminum as Furniture: Not Exactly
Your Basic Pots and Pans." *Oakland Tribune* (June
17, 1986), D: 8.

Giovannini 1986
Giovannini, Joseph. "Furnished by Their Own Four
Hands." *New York Times* (January 30, 1986),
C: 1, 10.

Giovannini 1986a
Giovannini, Joseph. "The Vanity, Mirroring Past
Glamour." *New York Times* (December 18, 1986),
C: 1.

Greenwich Time 1986
"Furniture Might Be Art but Is It Comfortable?"
Greenwich [Conn.] Time (September 25, 1986),
C: 4.

Harper and Hinds 1986
Harper, Paula, and Katherine Jannach Hinds.
*Contemporary Sculpture from the Martin Z.
Margulies Collection, Grove Isle, Coconut Grove,
Florida*. Privately printed, 1986.

Henry 1986
Henry, Gerrit. "New York Reviews: Wendell Castle/
Alexander Milliken." *Artnews* 85 (January 1986):
134.

Holmes 1986
Holmes, Roger. "Wendell Castle's Clocks: Time Is
Money." *Fine Woodworking* 59 (July/August 1986):
80–83.

Jacobson 1986
Jacobson, Sebby Wilson. "Wood with a Little Wit:
Wendell Castle and His Crew Bring a Whole New
Meaning to Furniture." *Rochester Times-Union*
(January 23, 1986), C: 3.

Koncius 1986
Koncius, Jura. "A Timely Switch from Furniture to
Art—Wendell Castle Turns His Talent to Highly
Stylized and Sculpted Time Pieces." *Washington
Post* (May 1, 1986), 1, 10.

Lewis 1986
Lewis, Jo Ann. "Sculpture That Works." *Washington
Post* (October 4, 1986), G: 2.

Lindquist 1986
Lindquist, Mark. *Sculpting Wood: Contemporary
Tools and Techniques*. Worcester, Mass.: Davis
Publications, 1986 (p. 68).

Lucie-Smith 1986
Lucie-Smith, Edward. "Time Capsules." *Artnews* 85
(March 1986): 110–114.

Mayer 1986
Mayer, Barbara. "Grandfather Clock More Than
Time-Keeping Device." *Greensboro [N.C.] News and
Record* (February 23, 1986).

Morch 1986
Morch, Al. "Heavy Aluminum." *San Francisco
Examiner* (June 14, 1986), B: 3.

Morgan 1986
Morgan, Robert. "There's Lots of Fun in Castle
Exhibition." *Rochester Democrat and Chronicle*
(January 26, 1986), D: 3.

Netsky 1986
Netsky, Ron. "Tasty Faculty Show at RIT." *Rochester
Democrat and Chronicle* (January 19, 1986), D: 3.

Netsky 1986a
Netsky, Ron. "Wendell Castle, Crossing the Line
That Separates Craftwork from Artwork." *Rochester
Democrat and Chronicle* (July 6, 1986), C: 1, 7–9.

Owings 1986
Owings, Robert. "Honors Bestowed at ACC
Conference." *American Craft* 46 (October/
November 1986): 6–8.

Pearlman 1986
Pearlman, Chee. "Perfect Timing." *Industrial Design*
33 (January/February 1986): 18–23, 63.

Peters 1986
Peters, Susan Dodge. "Artful Furniture." *Christian
Science Monitor* (April 8, 1986), 39.

Peters 1986a
Peters, Susan Dodge. "Review of Wendell Castle
Exhibit at MAG." *Rochester City Newspaper* (July
24, 1986), 19.

Peters 1986b
Peters, Susan Dodge. "Woodworking's New Shape."
Rochester City Newspaper (January 30, 1986), 19.

Schiffert 1986
Schiffert, Craig A. "Timely Masterpieces." *Pan Am
Clipper* (February 1986): 12.

Schiro 1986
Schiro, Anne-Marie. "Craft Museum Celebrates."
New York Times (October 21, 1986), B: 7.

Smith 1986
Smith, Patricia Beach. "Furniture Exhibit Lets
Aluminum Prove Its Mettle." *Sacramento [Calif.] Bee*
(June 26, 1986), C: 1.

Stone 1986
Stone, Michael A. *Contemporary American
Woodworkers*. Salt Lake City: Gibbs M. Smith,
1986 (pp. 114–129).

Tyndall 1986
Tyndall, Katie. "Sitting Pretty with Art Furniture." *Washington Times* (October 13, 1986): 64–65.

TWA Ambassador 1986
"Design—Time Keepers." *TWA Ambassador* (February 1986): 30.

Vanidades 1986
"Notas: Exposition de los mas Soprendentes." *Vanidades Continental* (February 18, 1986): 8.

Voell 1986
Voell, Paula. "Premier Designer: Wendell Castle Has His Own School for Craftsmen." *Buffalo News* (February 16, 1986), H: 1, 3.

Washington Uptown Citizen 1986
"Wendell Castle Clocks at the Renwick Gallery." *Washington Uptown Citizen* (January 19, 1986): 24.

1987

Fine Arts at Amherst 1987
"Exhibitions." *Fine Arts at Amherst [College], Newsletter of the Associates of Fine Arts* (Spring 1987): 1.

Bonetti 1987
Bonetti, David. "On and (Mostly) Off the Street." *Boston Phoenix* (January 27, 1987), C: 2.

Brighton-Pittsford Post 1987
"Wendell Castle Show Awes at Dawson." *Brighton-Pittsford [N.Y.] Post* (January 7, 1987).

Brighton-Pittsford Post 1987a
"Paley and Castle Offer Two-Man Show at RIT." *Brighton-Pittsford [N.Y.] Post* (March 4, 1987), B: 14.

Chicago Tribune 1987
"The Ultimate Steinway." *Chicago Tribune* (December 6, 1987).

Dishman 1987
Dishman, Laura Stewart. "Getting a Kick Out of Telling Time: New Clock for DuPont Centre More Than a Conversation Piece." *Orlando [Fla.] Sentinel* (October 4, 1987), F: 1.

Dormer 1987
Dormer, Peter. *The New Furniture: Trends and Traditions*. London: Thames and Hudson, 1987 (pp. 130, 139–140, figs. 144, 193–196).

Falk 1987
Falk, Sally. "Furniture as Art." *Indianapolis Star* (January 25, 1987), H: 1.

Ghent 1987
Ghent, Janet. "Castle's Current Mood Is Sheer Magic." *Oakland Tribune* (February 7, 1987), C: 1.

Giambruni 1987
Giambruni, Helen. "ACC's New Museum: Functional Craft to the Back of the Bus?" *Craft International* (April/May/June 1987): 20–21.

Hamm 1987
Hamm, Madeleine McDermott. "Art Furniture: Alive and Well in Houston." *Houston Chronicle* (March 12, 1987), E: 1.

Interior Design Market 1987
"Clocks: Wendell Castle's Clocks through Alexander F. Milliken." *Interior Design Market* (March 1987): 147.

Jacobson 1987
Jacobson, Sebby Wilson. "More Dream Castles: The Master of Funk and Function Shows Off His Wit in Wood Again." *Rochester Times-Union* (January 22, 1987), C: 3.

Jacobson 1987a
Jacobson, Sebby Wilson. "Style of the '80s: RIT Stirs Up the Spunk and the Funk of an Era That Hasn't Been Too Easy on the Eyes." *Rochester Times-Union* (March 30, 1987), C: 1, 4.

Jacobson 1987b
Jacobson, Sebby Wilson. "How Great Thine Art." *Rochester Times-Union* (October 7, 1987), C: 1–2.

Jacobson 1987c
Jacobson, Sebby Wilson. "Castle Making Steinway's Grandest Piano." *Rochester Times-Union* (October 30, 1987), C: 1.

Jacobson 1987d
Jacobson, Sebby Wilson. "WXXI Eyes the Business of Two Artists." *Rochester Times-Union* (November 25, 1987), C: 1.

Krebs 1987
Krebs, Betty Dietz. "Sculptor Featured in Dayton Art Institute." *Dayton Daily News and Journal Herald* (March 17, 1987), 36.

Lewis 1987
Lewis, Pamela. "Furniture: Tabling Questions of Art vs. Craft—Two Artists Make Statements in Utility." *Houston Post* (March 7, 1987), C: 1–2.

Long 1987
Long, Nancy. "Corporate Art: Combing Harlem and Soho for Major Works of Art." *Orlando [Fla.]* 41 (September 1987): 35–41.

McBride 1987
McBride, Elizabeth. "Exhibition Review." *Art Space* (Albuquerque) (Summer 1987): 67–68.

Meers 1987
Meers, Melinda. "Arts and Craft." *Rochester Democrat and Chronicle, Upstate Magazine* (July 6, 1987): 3.

Orlando Business Journal 1987
"DuPont Centre: Unexpected Home for the Fine Arts." *Grand Opening Dedication*, supplement to *Orlando [Fla.] Business Journal* 4 (December 13, 1987): 3.

Rochester Times-Union 1987
"Papal Seat Shows the Perils of Church Art." *Rochester Times-Union* (October 7, 1987), C: 1.

Scrivens 1987
Scrivens, Hugh. "Hugh Scrivens Looks at the World of Wendell Castle and His Students." *Woodworking International* (Summer 1987): 56–59.

Stapen 1987
Stapen, Nancy. "Bright Relief from Dull Weather." *Boston Herald* (January 16, 1987), W: 4.

Steward 1987
Steward, Laura. "Bold, Stylish, Classic: Newcomer Mixes Architectural Styles, Eras." *Orlando [Fla.] Sentinel* (December 17, 1987), D: 8.

Stimpson 1987
Stimpson, Miriam. *Modern Furniture Classics*. New York: Whitney Library/Watson-Guptill, 1987 (p. 174).

Tyler 1987
Tyler, Jan. "The Future of Time." *New York Newsday* (February 8, 1987): 46–51.

Wolfe 1987
Wolfe, Andrew D. "Furniture, Art, and Tourism Support One Another." *Brighton-Pittsford [N.Y.] Post* (September 23, 1987), B: 1, 3.

Woodworker 1987
"Nine American Woodworkers." *Woodworker* (October 1987): cover, 862–863.

1988

Ancona 1988
Ancona, Amy. "Castle at Carnegie." *ID, Magazine of International Design* (September/October 1988).

Anderson 1988
Anderson, Tanya. "Castle Gives Backyard Talk: Tradition in Transition Reveals Visual-Linguistic Changes." *Great Lakes Craft Journal* (July 1988): 1, 6, 13.

Aver 1988
Aver, James. "Craft or Art? Wendell Castle Furniture Is Both." *Milwaukee Journal* (July 20, 1988), E: 2.

Benson 1988
Benson, Robert. "Carving Out a Corporate Image." *Inland Architect* (May/June 1988): 40–41.

Brighton-Pittsford Post 1988
"Wendell Castle's Giant Clock Keeps Canadians on Time." *Brighton-Pittsford [N.Y.] Post* (November 16, 1988), B: 20.

Brown 1988
Brown, Patricia Leigh. "Currents: Not Just Grand, but 500 Grand." *New York Times* (May 26, 1988), C: 3.

Busch 1988
Busch, Akiko. "Surface, Nook, and Cranny." *Metropolis* (June 1988): 66–69.

Campbell 1988
Campbell, Mary. "Wendell Castle's Steinway Debuts at Carnegie Hall." *Rochester Democrat and Chronicle* (June 4, 1988), C: 20.

Chastain-Chapman 1988
Chastain-Chapman, Anthony Urbane. "Aspiring to History: The 'Eloquent Object' Exhibition Examines the Past to Define an Art in Craft Media." *American Craft* 48 (April/May 1988): 30–37, 91.

Chicago Tribune 1988
"Steinway No. 500,000." *Chicago Tribune* (June 4, 1988), 2: 7.

Craft 1988
Craft, Mary Anne. "Parallel Histories." *Corporate Art News* 5 (November 1988): 1.

Crafts Report 1988
"Wendell Castle to Build the 500,000th Steinway." *Crafts Report* (January 1988): 31.

Dowell 1988
Dowell, Susan Stiles. "Artful Juxtaposition: At Home with the Owners of Washington's Fendrick Gallery." *Southern Accents* (October 1988): 91–97.

Dowling and Solberg 1988
[Dowling, Claudio Glenn, and Sara Solberg]. "Ain't It Grand: Steinway & Sons Celebrates 135 Years of Celestial Sound by Building Its 500,000th Classic Piano." *Life* 11 (June 1988): 99–103.

Ferguson 1988
Ferguson, Bill. "Furniture Fantastique—Art Furniture, Designer Wendell Castle's Sought-After Creations Defy Traditional Definitions." *Syracuse [N.Y.] Herald-Journal* (April 25, 1988), C: 1–2.

Goodman 1988
Goodman, Peter. "In Praise of the Steinway." *New York Newsday* (June 4, 1988), 9, 18.

Hafner 1988
Hafner, Bev. "The New Renaissance of Art in Business." *Rochester Business Magazine* 4 (November 1988): 42–44.

Hartmann 1988
Hartmann, Donna. "Tour Set for Castle Works." *Woodshop News* (June 1988).

Hirst 1988
Hirst, Arlene. "The Late (Almost), Great (Maybe) '80's." *Metropolitan Home* 20 (November 1988): 114–118.

Howard 1988
Howard, Beth. "The Piano That's a Castle." *Metropolis* 8 (October 1988): 60–61.

Interior Design 1988
"Neocon 20 Special Issue." *Interior Design* 59 (May 1988): 92–93.

Jacobson 1988
Jacobson, Sebby Wilson. "More from the Castle Realm." *Rochester Times-Union* (January 14, 1988), C: 3.

Jacobson 1988a
Jacobson, Sebby Wilson. "Castle's Timely Work: A Clock for Toronto." *Rochester Times-Union* (February 5, 1988), C: 1, 14.

Jacobson 1988b
Jacobson, Sebby Wilson. "RIT Planning to Acquire Castle Wood School." *Rochester Times-Union* (February 19, 1988), C: 1.

Jacobson 1988c
Jacobson, Sebby Wilson. "Grand Opening: The Grandest of Grands. . . . " *Rochester Times-Union* (May 25, 1988), C: 1.

Jacobson 1988d
Jacobson, Sebby Wilson. "Only Two Other Great Grands in Steinway's History." *Rochester Times-Union* (May 25, 1988), C: 1–2.

Jacobson 1988e
Jacobson, Sebby Wilson. "Castle Piano Plays Well with Carnegie Proud." *Rochester Times-Union* (June 3, 1988), C: 1.

Jacobson 1988f
Jacobson, Sebby Wilson. "Demand for Castle Doesn't Stop with Steinway." *Rochester Times-Union* (June 9, 1988), C: 3.

Jacobson 1988g
Jacobson, Sebby Wilson. "Designer Steinway No. 500,000: It's Just Grand." *Bridgewater [N.J.] Courier-News* (June 13, 1988).

Jacobson 1988h
Jacobson, Sebby Wilson. "Sculptor Wins Money but Not Time—His Clock Is Stopped." *Rochester Times-Union* (September 29, 1988), C: 1.

Kimmelman 1988
Kimmelman, Michael. "Convention of Pianists Celebrates Steinway." *New York Times* (June 4, 1988), A: 10.

Kozinn 1988
Kozinn, Allen. "Pianists to Celebrate Steinway in Gala." *New York Times* (May 31, 1988), 18.

Kozinn 1988a
Kozinn, Allen. "Two Dozen Pianos Honor Steinway's 500,000th Creation." *Rochester Democrat and Chronicle* (June 3, 1988), C: 1.

Landis 1988
Landis, Dylan. "A Delicate Balance—Artist Wendell Castle Redefines Furniture and Does It with Humor." *Chicago Tribune* (March 27, 1988), 15: 3.

La Stampa 1988
"Il pianoforte Steinway numero 500 mila." *La Stampa* (Turin, Italy) (June 19, 1988).

Loukin 1988
Loukin, Andrea. "Limited Editions." *Interior Design Market* (October 1988).

McShane 1988
McShane, Larry. "Steinway Makes Pianos Works of Art." *Rochester Democrat and Chronicle* (May 27, 1988), C: 1, 5.

Morris 1988
Morris, Kathy. "Movers and Shakers in the Finger Lakes—Wendell Castle: The Art of Time in Wood." *Finger Lakes Magazine* (Ithaca, N.Y.) (Spring 1988): 28–29.

Morris 1988a
Morris, Kathy. "Artistry in Wood." *Finger Lakes Magazine* (Ithaca, N.Y.) (Fall 1988): 44–47.

Netsky 1988
Netsky, Ron. "Furniture with an English Accent: Two British Professors Bring the Flavor of Europe to the Wendell Castle School." *Rochester Democrat and Chronicle* (January 17, 1988), C: 3.

Netsky and Palmer 1988
Netsky, Ron, and Robert Palmer. "Wood Craft School Will Join RIT." *Rochester Democrat and Chronicle* (February 9, 1988), B: 1.

Palmer 1988
Palmer, Robert. "Timely Piece for Toronto." *Rochester Democrat and Chronicle* (September 28, 1988), C: 1.

Picht 1988
Picht, Randolph. "Artist Finds Niche between Worlds of Art and Furniture." *Ann Arbor [Mich.] News* (April 11, 1988), D: 3.

Picket 1988
Picket, Rudolph. "One Grand Affair." *Rochester Democrat and Chronicle* (May 27, 1988), C: 1, 5.

Rothstein 1988
Rothstein, Edward. "A Pianoforte Was His Forte." *Smithsonian* 19 (November 1988): 142–156.

Sedgewick 1988
Sedgewick, John. "Elements of Style: The Steinway Mystique." *GQ* (June 1988): 47, 55.

Swisher 1988
Swisher, Kara. "The Grandest of Them All." *Washington Post* (October 10, 1988), B: 1, 11.

Tagnini 1988/89
Tagnini, Joyce. "NEA Fellowships." *American Craft* 48 (December 1988/January 1989): 23.

Webster 1988
Webster, Daniel. "A Steinway Is Created in the Key of 'Gee!'" *Philadelphia Inquirer* (September 29, 1988), E: 1.

Yglesias 1988
Yglesias, Linda. "A Half Million Pianos Later." *New York Daily News* (May 15, 1988), 21–23.

1989

Fine Woodworking 1989
"Duet." *Fine Woodworking* 74 (January/February 1989): back cover.

Taragin 1989
Taragin, Davira S. "Evolution of a Commission: A Wendell Castle Bench." *Bulletin of the Detroit Institute of Arts* 65 (forthcoming).

1959

Lawrence 1959
Lawrence, Kansas, University of Kansas, Department of Design. "Sixth Annual Kansas Designer-Craftsman Exhibition." November 8–December 4, 1959.

1960

Kansas City 1960
Kansas City, Missouri, Nelson Gallery-Atkins Museum. "Mid-America Exhibition." March 31–April 30, 1960.

Omaha 1960
Omaha, Nebraska, Joslyn Art Museum. *Sixth Midwest Biennial Exhibition: Painting, Sculpture, Graphic Arts*. 1960.

Westwood 1960
Westwood, Kansas, Little Gallery and Frame Shop. "Wendell Castle." July 29–August 1960.

Wichita 1960
Wichita, Kansas, Wichita Art Association. "National Decorative Arts Show." 1960.

1962

Hanover 1962
Hanover, New Hampshire, Dartmouth College, Hopkins Center. "Inaugural Show." November 1962.

New York 1962
New York, Museum of Contemporary Crafts. *Young Americans 1962*. Jurors' statement by Robert Turner, Hedy B. Acklin, and John Griswold. 1962.

1963

Lawrence 1963
Lawrence, Kansas, University of Kansas, Union Building. "Tenth Annual Kansas Designer-Craftsman Exhibition." Fall 1963.

Rochester 1963
Rochester, New York, Rochester Public Library, Rundel Gallery. "William Sellers and Wendell Castle—RIT Faculty." Winter 1963.

Worcester and New York 1963
Worcester, Massachusetts, Worcester Art Museum, and New York, Museum of Contemporary Crafts. *Craftsmen of the Northeastern United States*. 1963.

1964

Andover 1964
Andover, Massachusetts, Phillips Academy, Addison Gallery of American Art. "Craftsmen outside New England." 1964.

Ithaca 1964
Ithaca, New York, Ithaca High School. "New York State Craft Fair." August 3–8, 1964.

Milan 1964
Milan, Italy. *United States of America at the Thirteenth Triennale of Milan*. 1964.

New York 1964
New York, American Craftsmen's Council at Columbia University. *First World Congress of Craftsmen*. Edited by Jacqueline Rice. 1964.

New York 1964a
New York, Museum of Contemporary Crafts. *The American Craftsman*. Introduction by Paul J. Smith. 1964.

New York 1964b
New York, Museum of Contemporary Crafts. *Amusements Is*. Statement by Paul J. Smith. 1964.

Rochester 1964
Rochester, New York, University of Rochester, Memorial Art Gallery. *Rochester–Finger Lakes Exhibition*. 1964.

Rochester 1964a
Rochester, New York, Shop One. "Wendell Castle: Recent Furniture." May 9–June 6, 1964.

Rochester 1964b
Rochester, New York, Rochester Institute of Technology, James E. Booth Memorial Building, Bevier Gallery. "Faculty Show." 1964.

1965

Champaign 1965
Champaign, Illinois, University of Illinois, Krannert Art Museum. *American Craftsmen/1965: Festival of Contemporary Arts*. Essay by R.v.N. 1965.

New York 1965
New York, United States Plywood Showroom. "Objects Illustrating Design in Wood Assembled by the Museum of Contemporary Crafts for U.S. Plywood." September 13–October 15, 1965.

Rochester 1965
Rochester, New York, University of Rochester, Memorial Art Gallery. *Rochester–Finger Lakes Exhibition*. 1965

Rochester 1965a
Rochester, New York, University of Rochester, Memorial Art Gallery. *Designed by Wendell Castle*. 1965.

EXHIBITION HISTORY

Compiled by Jennifer Way with assistance from Melanie Holcomb

Titles of exhibitions for which there is a catalogue are in *italic*.

1966

Chicago 1966
Chicago, University of Chicago, Renaissance Society. *Wendell Castle/Wharton Esherick/Sam Maloof/Marcelo Grassman*. 1966.

Hanover 1966
Hanover, New Hampshire, Dartmouth College, Hopkins Center, Beaumont-May Gallery. "Wendell Castle." July 2–14, 1966.

Mankato 1966
Mankato, Minnesota, Mankato State College. "Mankato Invitational." Fall 1966.

New York 1966
New York, Museum of Contemporary Crafts. *Fantasy Furniture*. 1966.

Rochester 1966
Rochester, New York, University of Rochester, Memorial Art Gallery. *Rochester–Finger Lakes Exhibition*. 1966.

San Francisco 1966
San Francisco, Museum West of the American Craftsmen's Council. "Woven Forms by Dominic DiMare—Furniture by Wendell Castle." September 13–October 23, 1966.

Stuttgart 1966
Stuttgart, Germany, Industrial Trade Board of Baden-Württemberg. "Internationales Kunsthandwerk, 1966." July 15–October 10, 1966.

Wilmington and New York 1966
Wilmington, Delaware, Delaware Art Center, and New York, American Craftsmen's Council. "Craftsmen USA '66: Northeast Regional Show." March 11–April 3, 1966. Exhibition circulated to New York, Museum of Contemporary Crafts, June 3–September 11, 1966.

1967

Laguna Beach 1967
Laguna Beach, California, Laguna Beach Art Association. *Media Explored 1967: An Invitational Exhibition*. Foreword by Dextra Frankel. 1967.

Louisville 1967
Louisville, Kentucky, Louisville Art Center Association. "Invitational Craft Exhibition." October 8–29, 1967.

Madison 1967
Madison, Wisconsin, Madison Art Association. "Regional Invitational Craft Show." December 10, 1967–January 14, 1968.

Muncie 1967
Muncie, Indiana, Ball State University Art Gallery. *Crafts 1967*. Preface by Paul J. Smith. 1967.

Spokane 1967
Spokane, Cheney Cowles Memorial Museum. "Northwest Craftsmen's Exhibition." November 21–December 24, 1967.

Syracuse 1967
Syracuse, New York, Syracuse University, Joe and Emily Lowe Art Gallery. *Design and Aesthetics in Wood*. 1967.

1968

New York 1968
New York, Lee Nordness Galleries. "Handcrafted Furniture by Wendell Castle—New York Debut." April 9–27, 1968.

New York 1968a
New York, Sachs Quality Stores, Eighth Avenue Branch. "An International Adventure in Advanced Seating Concepts." March 1968.

Normal 1968
Normal, Illinois, Illinois State University. *Second National Invitational Crafts Exhibition*. 1968.

Rochester 1968
Rochester, New York, Schuman Gallery. "Wendell Castle." November 1968.

St. Louis 1968
St. Louis, Famous-Barr Company, a Division of May Department Stores. "The Beautiful American: Contemporary Crafts USA." October 14–28, 1968.

Seattle 1968
Seattle, University of Washington, Henry Art Gallery. *The American Craftsmen's Invitational Exhibition*. Introduction by Gervais Reed. 1968.

1969

Brooklyn 1969
New York, Abraham & Straus. December 3, 1969.

Cortland 1969
Cortland, New York, State University of New York, Dowd Fine Arts Gallery. "University of Brockport Art Department Faculty." 1969.

Dekalb 1969
Dekalb, Illinois, Northern Illinois University, University Center Gallery. *The Faculty Collects: An Exhibition of Art Works Collected by the Faculty at Northern Illinois University at Dekalb*. 1969.

Dekalb 1969a
Dekalb, Illinois, Northern Illinois University, University Center Gallery. *First Annual Craft Invitational Exhibit*. 1969. Exhibition circulated to Ithaca, New York, Ithaca College Museum of Art, 1969.

Durham 1969
Durham, New Hampshire, University of New Hampshire, Scudder Gallery. "Wendell Castle." November 7–December 7, 1969.

Honolulu 1969
Honolulu Academy of Arts (cosponsored by the Museum of Contemporary Crafts, New York). "Excellence of the Object." February 27–April 6, 1969. Exhibition circulated to Oakland Museum, November 8–December 14, 1969; Trenton, New Jersey State Museum, January 17–March 8, 1970.

Ithaca 1969
Ithaca, New York, Ithaca College Museum of Art. *Zevi Blum and Wendell Castle*. 1969.

New York 1969
New York, Museum of Contemporary Crafts. "Objects USA: The Johnson Collection of Contemporary Crafts." Brochure. 1969. In cooperation with the United States Information Agency, the exhibition circulated to Washington, D.C., Smithsonian Institution, National Collection of Fine Arts, October 2–November 6, 1969; Rochester, New York, University of Rochester, Memorial Art Gallery, December 1969–January 1970; Bloomfield Hills, Michigan, Cranbrook Academy of Art, February 11–March 3, 1970; Cincinnati Art Museum, April 23–May 10, 1970; St. Paul Art Center, May 28–June 14, 1970; Seattle Art Museum, October 14–November 3, 1970; Los Angeles County Museum of Art, December 29, 1970–January 19, 1971.

Rochester 1969
Rochester, New York, Shop One. "Wendell Castle." November 14–December 1, 1969.

Terre Haute 1969
Terre Haute, Indiana, Indiana State University, Sheldon Swope Art Gallery. "Third Annual Invitational for Craftsmen." November 27, 1969–January 1, 1970.

Wichita 1969
Wichita, Kansas, Wichita Art Museum. *The Furniture of Wendell Castle*. Essay by Richard Stuart Teitz. 1969. Exhibition circulated to Lawrence, Kansas, University of Kansas, Museum of Art, July 11–August 24, 1969; Louisville, Kentucky, Louisville Art Center Association, September 3–23, 1969.

1970

Boston 1970
Boston City Hall Galleries. "Crafts 1970." March 16–April 17, 1970.

Durham 1970
Durham, New Hampshire, University of New Hampshire, Scudder Gallery. "Wendell Castle, Furniture Designer." November 5–December 5, 1970.

New York 1970
New York, Museum of Contemporary Crafts. "Contemplation Environments." January 20–March 8, 1970.

New York 1970a
New York, Lee Nordness Galleries. "Sculpted Furniture Forms." March 21–April 10, 1970.

Palo Alto 1970
Palo Alto, California, Sterling Associates. "Furniture as Works of Art II." December 14, 1970–January 29, 1971.

Rockford 1970
Rockford, Illinois, Burpee Art Museum. *Art in Other Media: Ceramic, Glass, Textile, Wood.* 1970.

Trenton 1970
Trenton, New Jersey State Museum. *Contemporary Crafts.* Preface by Zoltan Buki. 1970.

1971

Binghamton 1971
Binghamton, New York, State University of New York, Art Gallery. *Master Craftsmen: An Invitational Exhibition.* 1970.

Buffalo 1971
Buffalo, Gallery West. "Nancy Jurs—Wendell Castle." October 8–31, 1971.

1972

Albany 1972
Albany, New York, State University of New York, University Art Gallery. *New York State Craftsmen: 1972 Selection.* Essay by Kenneth M. Wilson. 1972.

New York 1972
New York, Gallery Gimbels East. "Wendell Castle." February 1972.

New York and Washington 1972
New York, Museum of Contemporary Crafts. *Objects for Preparing Food.* Essays by Sandra K. Zimmerman, Mimi Sheraton, and Yukehisa Isobe. 1972. Exhibition circulated to Washington, D.C., Smithsonian Institution, National Collection of Fine Arts, Renwick Gallery, February 9–April 29, 1973.

Palo Alto 1972
Palo Alto, California, Sterling Associates. December 7, 1972–January 29, 1973.

Rochester 1972
Rochester, New York, Shop One. "Five Owners." April 3–29, 1972.

Rochester 1972a
Rochester, New York, Xerox Square Exhibit Center. "Radial 80." January 22–March 10, 1972.

Washington 1972
Washington, D.C., Smithsonian Institution, National Collection of Fine Arts, Renwick Gallery. *Woodenworks: Furniture Objects by Five Contemporary Craftsmen—George Nakashima, Sam Maloof, Wharton Esherick, Arthur Espenet Carpenter, Wendell Castle.* 1972. Exhibition circulated to St. Paul, Minnesota Museum of Art, October 12–December 31, 1972.

1973

Baltimore 1973
Baltimore, Nostalgia et Cetera Galleries. "Couples." 1973.

La Jolla 1973
La Jolla, California, La Jolla Museum of Contemporary Art. *Innovations: Contemporary Home Environments.* Introduction by Jay Belloli. 1973.

Milan 1973
Milan, Italy. "Sixteenth Triennale." September 20–November 20, 1973.

New York 1973
New York, Fairtree Gallery of Contemporary Crafts. *Paley/Castle.* 1973. Exhibition circulated to Philadelphia, Temple University, Tyler School of Art, November 30–December 16, 1973; Ithaca, New York, Cornell University, Herbert F. Johnson Museum of Art, January 23–February 27, 1974.

Rochester 1973
Rochester, New York, Xerox Square Exhibit Center. "Fun and Fantasy '74." November 8–December 30, 1973. Exhibition circulated to New York, Fairtree Gallery of Contemporary Crafts, January 12–February 16, 1974.

1974

Binghamton 1974
Binghamton, New York, State University of New York, Roberson Center for the Arts and Sciences. *The Fine Art of Craftsmanship.* Introduction by Roslyn Tunis. 1974.

Edinboro 1974
Edinboro, Pennsylvania, Edinboro State College, Bruce Gallery. "Nine Artisans." February 19–March 15, 1974.

Philadelphia 1974
Philadelpia, Richard Kagan Studio and Gallery. "Seven Woodworkers." April 18–June 1, 1974.

Rochester 1974
Rochester, New York, University of Rochester, Memorial Art Gallery. "Sitzart." July–September 1974.

Rochester 1974a
Rochester, New York, Shop One. "Wendell Castle Woodenworks." April 17–May 8, 1974.

Rochester 1974b
Rochester, New York, Xerox Square Exhibit Center. "Radial 80." February 23–April 5, 1974.

Toronto 1974
Toronto, Ontario Science Center and the World Crafts Council. *In Praise of Hands* (published in conjunction with the "First World Crafts Exhibition"). Foreword by James S. Plaut, essay by Octavio Paz. 1974.

1975

Buffalo 1975
Buffalo, State University of New York, Burchfield Center. *Language of Wood: Buffalo Craftsmen and the Burchfield Center Present Twenty-nine North American Designer-Craftsmen.* Introduction by Edna M. Lindemann, essay by Wesley F. Brett. 1975.

Cleveland 1975
Cleveland, Case Western Reserve University, Mather Gallery. "The Craftsman as Sculptor." October 31–November 18, 1975.

Lincoln 1975
Lincoln, Massachusetts, De Cordova and Dana Museum and Park. *Bed and Board: Contemporary Quilts and Woodwork.* Foreword by Frederick P. Walkey. 1975.

New York 1975
New York Coliseum. *Third Annual International Craft Show and Fair.* 1975.

Rochester 1975
Rochester, New York, Rochester Institute of Technology. *Faculty and Alumni Exhibition, Twenty-fifth Anniversary, School for American Craftsmen.* 1975.

Toronto 1975
Toronto, Art Gallery of Ontario. *Chairs.* Introduction by Alvin Balkind. 1975.

Washington 1975
Washington, D.C., Smithsonian Institution, National Collection of Fine Arts, Renwick Gallery. *Craft Multiples*. Essays by Lloyd E. Herman, Miriam Davidson Plotnicou, and Lois Moran. Exhibition circulated until 1979.

1976

Chicago 1976
Chicago, Museum of Contemporary Art. *American Crafts '76: An Aesthetic View*. Foreword by Stephen Prokopoff, introduction by Bernard Kester. 1976.

Kansas City 1976
Kansas City, Missouri, Kansas City Art Institute, Charlotte Crosby Kemper Gallery. "Invitational Crafts: Wood, Fiber, Clay." February 20–March 7, 1976.

New York 1976
New York, Beylerian Ltd. "Wendell Castle and Rinaldo Fratolillo." June 1976.

Philadelphia 1976
Philadelphia, Civic Center. *Forty-first International Eucharistic Congress Exhibition of Liturgical Arts*. 1976.

Philadelphia 1976a
Philadelphia, Richard Kagan Studio and Gallery. "Hardwood Furniture and Objects: Winter 1976." January 31–March 28, 1976.

1977

Philadelphia 1977
Philadelphia, Richard Kagan Studio and Gallery. "Six American Furniture Craftsmen." August 1977.

Philadelphia 1977a
Philadelphia, Richard Kagan Studio and Gallery. "Tables: New Variations: A Diversity of Uses and Designs for the Functional Flat Surface." October 2–24, 1977.

Philadelphia 1977b
Philadelphia, Richard Kagan Studio and Gallery. "Wood/Spirit/Form: A National Exhibition of Major Contemporary Woodworkers." October 29–December 31, 1977.

Philadelphia 1977c
Philadelphia Museum of Art. *American Crafts 1977*. Essay by Elena Karina Canavier. 1977. Exhibition circulated to Philadelphia Memorial Hall, Philadelphia Craft Show, November 3–6, 1977.

Rochester 1977
Rochester, New York, Rochester Institute of Technology. "Drawing Exhibition." 1977.

Washington 1977
Washington, D.C., Fendrick Gallery. *The American Table*. 1977.

1978

Baltimore 1978
Baltimore, Hopkins Plaza, Mechanic Theater. 1978.

Boston 1978
Boston, Museum of Fine Arts. "Contemporary Works by Master Craftsmen." 1978.

Cape Girardeau 1978
Cape Girardeau, Missouri, Southeast Missouri State University, University Gallery. "Invitational Wood Sculpture Exhibition." March 1978.

Newport 1978
Newport, Rhode Island, Cooper and French Gallery. "American Craftsmen Salute the America's Cup." May 1978.

New York 1978
New York, Carl Solway Gallery. "Illusions." May 9–June 3, 1978.

Philadelphia 1978
Philadelphia, Richard Kagan Studio and Gallery. "Wood: Traditions/Innovations, Furniture and Objects by Fourteen American Woodworkers." November 3–December 17, 1978.

Sanborn 1978
Sanborn, New York, Niagara County Community College. *Fantasy '78*. 1978.

Sheboygan 1978
Sheboygan, Wisconsin, John Michael Kohler Arts Center. *American Chairs—Form, Function, and Fantasy*. Essay by Naomi Gilman. 1978.

Vatican City 1978
Vatican City, Monumenti Musei, Galleria Pontificie. "Craft, Art and Religion." July 11–September 15, 1978.

Washington 1978
Washington, D.C., Fendrick Gallery. "Furniture as Art." October 10–November 4, 1978.

Worcester 1978
Worcester, Massachusetts, Craft Center. *Sixteen American Woodcarvers*. Exhibition circulated to New York, Warner Communications, April 3–28, 1978.

1979

New York 1979
New York, American Craft Museum. *New Handmade Furniture: American Furniture Makers Working in Hardwood*. Statement by Paul J. Smith. Exhibition circulated to West Palm Beach, Florida, Norton Gallery of Art, May 28–July 6, 1980.

New York 1979a
New York, Elements Gallery. "Architectural Dimensions." September 11–October 20, 1979.

New York 1979b
New York, Bowery Savings Bank. May–June 1979.

Philadelphia 1979
Philadelphia, Richard Kagan Studio and Gallery. "Hardwood Furniture and Objects: Fall '79." September 8–30, 1979.

Philadelphia 1979a
Philadelphia, Richard Kagan Studio and Gallery. "More Wood: An Exhibition of Smaller Pieces." November 3–December 9, 1979.

Rochester 1979
Rochester, New York, University of Rochester, Memorial Art Gallery. *Paley/Castle/Wildenhain*. Essay by Bruce W. Chambers. 1979.

Verona 1979
Verona, Pennsylvania, Society for Art in Crafts. *Art in Modern Handcrafts*. Essay by Elizabeth Raphael. 1979. Exhibition circulated to Pittsburgh, Carnegie Museum of Art, July 5–September 16, 1979.

1980

Atlanta 1980
Atlanta, American Gallery. "Wood and Iron Invitational '80." November 8–28, 1980.

Atlanta 1980a
Atlanta, Colony Square. "America at Its Best: Wood and Iron." November 22–December 16, 1980.

Boston 1980
Boston, Society of Arts and Crafts. "Sitting in Style: Wendell Castle, Tage Frid, Judy Kensley McKie, Contemporary Furniture in Cooperation with the Museum of Fine Arts." May 18–June 30, 1980.

Cambridge 1980
Cambridge, Massachusetts, Ten Arrow Gallery. "Wendell Castle." March 23–April 26, 1980.

Dayton 1980
Dayton Art Institute, Experiencenter. *Woodworks I: New American Sculpture*. Essay by Pamela Houk. 1980.

Louisville 1980
Louisville, Kentucky, Louisville Art Gallery at the Hyatt Regency. "Contemporary Furniture: Wood and Iron." September 15–26, 1980.

New York 1980
New York, National Fine Arts Committee of the Thirteenth Olympic Games at the American Craft Museum. "Art for Use." January–May 25, 1980.

Philadelphia 1980
Philadelphia, Richard Kagan Studio and Gallery. "Hardwood Furniture and Objects: Fall '80." October 18–November 9, 1980.

Washington 1980
Washington, D.C., Fendrick Gallery. "Furniture as Art II." November 5–29, 1980.

Washington 1980a
Washington, D.C., Greenwood Gallery. *Inaugural Exhibition*. 1980.

1981

Atlanta 1981
Atlanta, American Gallery. "Sculptural Furniture 1981." November 8–28, 1981.

Bay Harbor Island 1981
Bay Harbor Island, Florida, Medici-Berenson Gallery. "Wood Show." November 12–December 8, 1981.

Brockport 1981
Brockport, New York, State University of New York, Tower Fine Arts Gallery. "Faculty Show." November 14–December 18, 1981.

East Hampton 1981
East Hampton, New York, Pritam and Eames Gallery. "Opening Exhibit—Pritam and Eames." May 1981.

Galveston 1981
Galveston, Texas, Galveston Arts Center on the Strand. "Thirty Americans—An Invitational Exhibition: Clay, Fiber, Glass, Metal, Wood." June 5–28, 1981.

New York 1981
New York, Alexander F. Milliken. "Wendell Castle: Sculpture." January 3–28, 1981.

New York 1981a
New York, American Craft Museum. "Beyond Tradition: Twenty-fifth Anniversary Exhibition." October 1, 1981–January 1982.

New York 1981b
New York, Pratt Manhattan Center Gallery. *For Love and Money: Dealers Choose*. Introduction by Ellen Schwartz. 1981. Exhibition circulated to Brooklyn, Pratt Institute Gallery, October 22–November 25, 1981.

Philadelphia 1981
Philadelphia, Richard Kagan Studio and Gallery. "The Growth of a Tradition: Fifteen Woodworkers." April 11–May 3, 1981.

Rochester 1981
Rochester, New York, Junior League of Rochester. "Decorators' Show House III." May 2–24, 1981.

Rochester 1981a
Rochester, New York, University of Rochester, Memorial Art Gallery. *The Fine Art of the Furniture Maker: Conversations with Wendell Castle, Artist, and Penelope Hunter-Stiebel, Curator, about Selected Works from the Metropolitan Museum of Art* (published in conjunction with the exhibition "The Fine Art of the Furniture Maker"). Edited by Patricia Bayer. 1981.

1982

Chautauqua 1982
Chautauqua, New York, Chautauqua Association Galleries. "Twenty-fifth Annual Chautauqua National Exhibition." June–July 1982.

Columbia 1982
Columbia, South Carolina, Columbia Museum of Art and Science. "Invitational Wood and Fiber." November 27, 1982–January 2, 1983.

East Hampton 1982
East Hampton, New York, Pritam and Eames Gallery. "Work from the Masters." May–June 1982.

New York 1982
New York, Gunlocke Showroom. "Designer's Saturday, Imagination, Reality: Gunlocke, Wendell Castle." Pamphlet. 1982.

Niagara Falls 1982
Niagara Falls, New York, Niagara University, Buscaglia Castellani Art Gallery. "Recent Art Furniture: Survey of Current Art Furniture in the Northeast." May 14–June 14, 1982.

Philadelphia 1982
Philadelphia, Richard Kagan Studio and Gallery. "Hardwood Furniture/Objects: Spring '82." April 10–May 2, 1982.

Washington 1982
Washington, D.C. (Georgetown). "Decorators' Show House." Fall 1982.

Worcester 1982
Worcester, Massachusetts, Worcester Craft Center. "New Views in Furniture: The Northeast." 1982.

1983

Chicago 1983
Chicago, Gunlocke Showroom. "National Exposition of Interior Contract Furnishings" (NEOCON). June 14–17, 1983.

Cincinnati 1983
Cincinnati, Taft Museum. *Material Illusion: Unlikely Material*. Statement by Heather Hallenberd. 1983.

East Hampton 1983
East Hampton, New York, Pritam and Eames Gallery. "The Desk." August–October 1983.

Los Angeles 1983
Los Angeles, Gunlocke Showroom. "West Week." April 1983.

New York 1983
New York, Alexander F. Milliken. "The Extraordinary Art of Wendell Castle." March 8–April 20, 1983.

New York 1983a
New York, Gunlocke Showroom. "Designer's Saturday." October 13–15, 1983.

New York 1983b
New York, Steelcase, Inc. "Evolution of the Workspace." August 22–October 15, 1983.

New York 1983c
New York, Alexander F. Milliken. "Eight Realists." Brochure. April 30–June 1, 1983.

Philadelphia 1983
Philadelphia, Richard Kagan Studio and Gallery. "Tenth Anniversary Celebration: 1974–1983." April 1983.

Rockville 1983
Rockville, Maryland, Montgomery College, Art Gallery. "Woodworking Invitational." March 21–April 15, 1983.

St. Louis 1983
St. Louis, Craft Alliance. *National Wood Invitational*. Statement by Horty Schreiber. 1983.

Washington 1983
Washington, D.C., Fendrick Gallery. "American Living National Treasures." May 14–June 18, 1983.

Yonkers 1983
Yonkers, New York, Hudson River Museum. *Ornamentalism: The New Decorativeness in Architecture and Design*. 1983. Exhibition circulated to Austin, University of Texas, Archer M. Huntington Art Gallery, September 1–October 16, 1983.

1984

Boston 1984
Boston, Ten Arrow Gallery. "Furniture from the Wendell Castle School." February 17–March 29, 1984.

Boston 1984a
Boston, Harcus Gallery. "Ornamentalism." December 1984.

Dallas 1984
Dallas, Gunlocke Showroom. "Contract Designers Show" (CONDES). January 1984.

East Hampton 1984
East Hampton, New York, Pritam and Eames Gallery. "An Exhibition of Desks and Chairs." August–October 1984.

Houston 1984
Houston, Gunlocke Showroom. June 1984.

New York 1984
New York, Alexander F. Milliken. "The School of Wendell Castle: The Art of Handmade Furniture." May 19–June 6, 1984.

New York 1984a
New York, Arc International, Gallery of Applied Arts. "Opening Installation: The Arc Collection." October 1984.

New York 1984b
New York, Gallery at Workbench and the Formica Corporation. *Material Evidence: New Color Techniques in Handmade Furniture*. Essays by Bernice Wollman, Judy Coady, Susan Grant Lewis, and Lloyd Herman. 1984. Exhibition circulated by Smithsonian Institution Traveling Exhibition Service to Washington, D.C., Smithsonian Institution, National Museum of American Art, Renwick Gallery, and Dayton Art Institute.

New York 1984c
New York, Alexander F. Milliken. "Group Exhibition." December 8, 1984–January 9, 1985.

Philadelphia 1984
Philadelphia, Helen Drutt Gallery. 1984.

1985

Athens 1985
Athens, Ohio, Southeastern Ohio Cultural Arts Center, Dairy Barn Gallery. *American Contemporary Works in Wood '85*. September 12–October 20, 1985.

Austin 1985
Austin, Texas, Laguna Gloria Art Museum. *Tradition and Innovation: Decorative Art by Castle, Chihuly, Paley, Woodman*. Introduction by Bernice Collins Torregrossa. 1985.

Cincinnati 1985
Cincinnati, Taft Museum. *Masterpieces of Time*. 1985. Exhibition circulated to New York, Alexander F. Milliken, November 2–December 20, 1985; Washington, D.C., Smithsonian Institution, National Museum of American Art, Renwick Gallery, December 24, 1985–May 4, 1986.

Geneseo 1985
Geneseo, New York, State University of New York, Bertha V. B. Lederer Fine Arts Gallery. "Invitational Exhibit: Clay, Fiber, Metal, Wood." February 8–March 2, 1985.

New York 1985
New York, Whitney Museum of American Art. *High Styles: Twentieth-Century American Design*. 1985.

Philadelphia 1985
Philadelphia, Snyderman Gallery. "Contemporary American Woodworkers." December 8, 1985–January 19, 1986.

Rochester 1985
Rochester, New York, Rochester Institute of Technology, James E. Booth Memorial Building, Bevier Gallery. "Faculty Exhibition." February 1985.

San Angelo 1985
San Angelo, Texas, San Angelo Museum of Fine Arts. "New Chair." May 31–June 30, 1985. Exhibition circulated to Corpus Christi, Texas, Art Museum of South Texas, July 8–August 30, 1985; Breckenridge, Texas, Breckenridge Fine Arts Museum, November 25, 1985–January 2, 1986; Raleigh, North Carolina, North Carolina State University, School of Design, March 31–April 24, 1986.

Washington 1985
Washington, D.C., Fendrick Gallery. "The School of Wendell Castle: Handmade Furniture/Sculptural Forms." June 20–September 2, 1985.

1986

East Hampton 1986
East Hampton, New York, Pritam and Eames Gallery. "Art at Home." July–August 1986.

Lincroft 1986
Lincroft, New Jersey, Monmouth Museum. *Contemporary Arts: An Expanding View*. Guest curator Helen W. Drutt English. 1986. Exhibition circulated to Princeton, New Jersey, Squibb Gallery, October 1–November 2, 1986.

New York 1986
New York, Alexander F. Milliken. "Group Exhibition." January 4–29, 1986.

New York 1986a
New York, Alexander F. Milliken. "More Recent Work." September 13–October 10, 1986.

New York 1986b
New York, American Craft Museum. *Craft Today: Poetry of the Physical*. Essay by Paul J. Smith and Edward Lucie-Smith. 1986. Exhibition circulated to Denver Art Museum, May 16–July 15, 1987; Laguna Beach, California, Laguna Beach Art Museum, August 7–October 4, 1987; Phoenix Art Museum, November 7, 1987–January 10, 1988; Milwaukee Art Museum, February 12–April 10, 1988; Louisville, Kentucky, J. B. Speed Art Museum, May 16–July 10, 1988; Richmond, Virginia, Virginia Museum of Fine Arts, August 9–October 2, 1988.

New York 1986c
New York, Alexander F. Milliken. "New Work/Sculpture." June 14–July 18, 1986.

Oakland 1986
Oakland, Kaiser Center Art Gallery. "Furniture in the Aluminum Vein." May 30–July 11, 1986.

Philadelphia 1986
Philadelphia, Snyderman Gallery. "The Wendell Castle School: Designer-Crafted Furniture and Sculpture." December 7, 1986–January 16, 1987.

Rochester 1986
Rochester, New York, University of Rochester, Memorial Art Gallery. *Time and Defiance of Gravity: Recent Works of Wendell Castle*. Essay by Lisa Hammel. 1986. Exhibition circulated to Amherst, Massachusetts, Amherst College, Mead Art Museum, October 1–November 9, 1986.

Rochester 1986a
Rochester, New York, Oxford Gallery. *Celebrating Twenty-five Years: 1961–1986*. 1986.

Rochester 1986b
Rochester, New York, Dawson Gallery. "Wendell Castle Faculty Show." January 9–February 10, 1986.

Rochester 1986c
Rochester, New York, Rochester Institute of Technology, James E. Booth Memorial Building, Bevier Gallery. "Faculty Exhibition." February 1986.

Toronto 1986
Toronto, Twentieth-Century Gallery. "Wendell Castle: Works in Plastic, 1968–1970." September 27–October 25, 1986.

Verona 1986
Verona, Pennsylvania, Society for Art in Crafts. *The Store 1972–1985: Selected Works*. Text by Florence Rosner. 1986.

Washington 1986
Washington, D.C., Fendrick Gallery. "Wendell Castle. Sculpture? Furniture? The Vanishing Line." September 17–October 18, 1986.

1987

Boston 1987
Boston, Harcus Gallery. "Wendell Castle: Most Recent Sculpture." January 7–February 7, 1987.

Chicago 1987
Chicago, Alexander F. Milliken. *Chicago International New Art Forms Exposition*. 1987.

East Hampton 1987
East Hampton, New York, Pritam and Eames Gallery. "Early Spring Show." 1987.

Houston 1987
Houston, Judy Youens Perception Galleries. "Wendell Castle. New Work/Sculpture." March 11–April 25, 1987.

Indianapolis 1987
Indianapolis, Center for Contemporary Arts, Herron Gallery. *The Furniture Show: Contemporary Lamps, Tables by Furniture-Makers/Artists*. 1987.

New Canaan 1987
New Canaan, Connecticut, Silvermine Guild Arts Center, "Explicitly Ornamental." October 17–November 15, 1987. Exhibition circulated to Stamford, Connecticut, Metro Center, December 9–30, 1987.

New York 1987
New York, Alexander F. Milliken. "New Work: Wendell Castle, Garry Knox Bennett, Fred Baier." September 12–October 14, 1987.

New York 1987a
New York, Bowery Savings Bank. May–July 1987.

Portland 1987
Portland, Oregon, Contemporary Crafts Gallery. "Fiftieth Anniversary, Wood." July 12–August 6, 1987.

Purchase 1987
Purchase, New York, Pepsico, Inc. "Selections from the Permanent Collection of the American Craft Museum." July–August 1987.

Rochester 1987
Rochester, New York, Rochester Institute of Technology, James E. Booth Memorial Building, Bevier Gallery. "An Exhibition of Works by Albert Paley and Wendell Castle, Artists-in-Residence in the School for American Craftsmen." 1987.

Rochester 1987a
Rochester, New York, Dawson Gallery. "Second Annual Wendell Castle Faculty Show." January 9–February 10, 1987.

Rochester 1987b
Rochester, New York, Rochester Institute of Technology, James E. Booth Memorial Building, Bevier Gallery. "Faculty Exhibition." 1987.

Tulsa 1987
Tulsa, Philbrook Museum of Art. *The Eloquent Object: The Evolution of American Art in Craft Media since 1945*. Edited by Marcia Manhart and Tom Manhart. 1987. Exhibition circulated to Oakland Museum, February 20–March 15, 1988; Boston, Museum of Fine Arts, July 6–August 28, 1988; Chicago Public Library Cultural Center, September 24–December 30, 1988; Orlando, Florida, Orlando Museum of Art, March 19–May 14, 1989; Richmond, Virginia, Virginia Museum of Fine Arts, June 27–August 20, 1989.

1988

Brockport 1988
Brockport, New York, State University of New York. "Public Art: Making a Better Place to Live." November 15–December 11, 1988.

Cambridge 1988
Cambridge, Massachusetts, Ten Arrow Gallery. "Wendell Castle School." February 1988.

Chicago 1988
Chicago. *Chicago International New Art Forms Exposition*. 1988.

Chicago 1988a
Chicago, Hokin/Kaufman Gallery. "The Art of Wendell Castle." March 25–April 23, 1988.

Grosse Pointe 1988
Grosse Pointe, Michigan, Joy Emery Gallery. "The Art of Design." November 10–December 31, 1988.

Milwaukee 1988
Milwaukee, Marquette University, Patrick and Beatrice Haggerty Museum of Art. "Furniture/Furniture: The New Styles." June 3–July 17, 1988.

Milwaukee 1988a
Milwaukee Art Museum. *1988: The World of Art Today*. Essay by Dawn von Wiegand. 1988.

New York 1988
New York, Lexington Armory. "Art at the Armory." January 24–February 1, 1988.

New York 1988a
New York, Alexander F. Milliken. "Group Exhibition." September 12–October 14, 1988.

New York 1988b
New York, Alexander F. Milliken. "Wendell Castle: A Decade 1977–1987." November 19–December 23, 1988.

New York 1988c
New York, Alexander F. Milliken. "Wendell Castle: New Work/Sculpture." June 14–July 18, 1988.

Philadelphia 1988
Philadelphia, Drexel University, Nesbitt College of Design Arts. "Tradition in Transition: Recent Works by Wendell Castle." October 31–November 11, 1988.

Providence 1988
Providence, Rhode Island, Rhode Island School of Design, Museum of Art. *1900 to Now: Modern Art from Rhode Island Collections*. 1988.

Rochester 1988
Rochester, New York, Dawson Gallery. "Third Annual Wendell Castle Faculty Show." January 8–February 9, 1988.

Rochester 1988a
Rochester, New York, Rochester Institute of Technology, James E. Booth Memorial Building, Bevier Gallery. "College of Fine and Applied Arts Faculty Show." 1988.

PHOTOGRAPH CREDITS

The color photographs reproduced in this book are by Dirk Bakker, Detroit Institute of Arts. Unless otherwise noted, black-and-white photographs were supplied by the owners of the work reproduced. Photographs of figs. 3, 8, 9, and 11–21 were supplied by the artist. Individual photographers are acknowledged below:

Geoffrey Clements: fig. 26; Jenny Clifton: fig. 1; Joe Coscia, Jr.: fig. 28; John A. Ferrari: fig. 6; Ted Kawalewski: fig. 14; Bruce Miller: figs. 19–21; Michael Moran: fig. 29; Otto E. Nelson: fig. 2; Steven Sloman: figs. 6, 11, and 15; Tim Street-Porter: fig. 24.